SADLIER
FAITH AND
WITNESS

CREED

A Course
on Catholic Belief
Part II

Norman F. Josaitis, S.T.D.

Rev. Michael J. Lanning, O.F.M.

William H. Sadlier, Inc.
9 Pine Street
New York, New York 10005-1002
http://www.sadlier.com

Acknowledgments

Scripture selections are taken from the *New American Bible* Copyright © 1991, 1986, 1970 by the Confraternity of Christian Doctrine, Washington, D.C. and are used by license of the copyright owner. All rights reserved. No part of the *New American Bible* may be used or reproduced in any form, without permission in writing from the copyright owner.

Excerpts from the English translation of the *Catechism of the Catholic Church* for use in the United States of America, Copyright © 1994, United States Catholic Conference, Inc.—Libreria Editrice Vaticana. Used with permission.

Excerpts from the English translation of *The Roman Missal* © 1973, International Committee on English in the Liturgy, Inc. (ICEL); excerpts from the English translation of *Rite of Penance* © 1974, ICEL; excerpts from the English translation of *Dedication of a Church and An Altar* © 1978, ICEL; excerpts from the English translation of *A Book of Prayers* © 1982, ICEL. All rights reserved.

English translation of the Our Father, Apostles' Creed, and Nicene Creed by the International Consultation on English Texts, (ICET).

Excerpts from *Catholic Household Blessings and Prayers* © 1988, United States Catholic Conference, Washington, D.C. All rights reserved.

Excerpts from *The Documents of Vatican II*, Walter M. Abbott, S.J., General Editor, © 1966 by American Press, Inc. 106 West 56th Street, New York, NY 10019. Used with permission. All rights reserved.

Excerpt from *Praying with Hildegard of Bingen* by Gloria Durka (Winona, MN: Saint Mary's Press, 1991). Used by permission of the publisher. All rights reserved.

Excerpt from *Saints for All Seasons* by John J. Delaney. Copyright © 1978 by John J. Delaney. Used by permission of Doubleday, a division of Bantam Doubleday Dell Publishing Group, Inc.

Cover Illustrator: Diane Fenster

Jim Saylor
Photo Editor

Lori Berkowitz
Photo Researcher

Cover Photos

Art Resource: back cover, center. *The Crosiers/* Gene Plaisted, OSC: front cover, bottom left; front cover, top right. *Anne Hamersky:* back cover, top left.

Photo Credits

ABC Studios: 83 left.
Adventure Photo and Film: Michael Powers: 14; Barbara Brown: 107.
Animals Animals/ E.R. Degginger: 24–25.
Art Resource: 26; Erich Lessing: 88–89.
Borland Stock Photo/ C. Borland: 98; Jerry Selmack: 111.
Kevin Butler: 11, 60–61, 106–107 background.
Catholic News Service: 67; Charles Schisla: 53; Bob Roller: 61 bottom; Michael Edrington: 110.
Dwight Cendrowski: 83 right.
Comstock: 40–41 basilica.
The Crosiers/ Gene Plaisted, OSC: 13, 36, 61 top, 62, 66, 69 left, 75, 82, 83 bottom, 100, 101 all.
Leo de Wys/ Sipa: 20–21 hands, 40–41 hands; Riclafe: 118–119.
Don Eastman: 22 top.
Dana Edmunds: 115.
FPG/ Bob Peterson: 92; Telegraph Colour Library: 124–125.
Franciscan Missionaries of Mary: 77.
Benedictine Sisters of Perpetual Adoration: 76 top.
The Image Bank/ Grant Faint: 99; Alexander Stewart: 116–117.
Ken Karp: 68.
L'osservatore Romano/ Catholic Near East Magazine: 85.

Liaison International/ Sheila Beougher: 42 center; Noel: 54 right; F. Lo Chon: 54 left; A. Georgeon: 78; Anticoli Luvio: 104–105.
National Geographic Society/ Paul Chesley: 56–57.
Nonstock/ Kristofer Dan-Bergman: 70.
Palm Beach Post/ John Lopinot: 38 top right; Loren Hosack: 43.
Photo Edit/ Alan Oddie: 12.
Photonica/ Kazuyuki Hashimoto: 46; Mel Curtis: 90–91.
Photo Researchers/ David Nunuck: 112–113.
Picture Perfect: 37; K. Schlea: 28.
Frances Roberts: 38 bottom left.
Chris Sheridan: 69 right, 76 bottom, 117.
Jacqueline Srouji: 61 center.
Stock Imagery/ Kaiser: 50.
Stock Market/ Stocknet: 8–9; Peter Steiner: 29; Bilderberg: 58.
Superstock/ Gerard Fritz: 44–45; Kris Coppieters: 108.
SYGMA/ G. Giansanti: 48–49, 64–65, 72–73.
Tony Stone Images: 42 background; Danny Torckler: 7; Michael Busselle: 16–17; Hulton Getty: 18; Rich Frishman: 22 bottom; J. Szkodzinski: 32–33; Bruce Ayres: 34; Bob Daemmrich: 38 bottom right; Brian Bailey: 74; Traveler's Resource: 80–81; Vera Storman: 94; Larry Ulrich: 96–97; Chris Simpson: 97; Patricia Thompson: 109.
Larry Ulrich: 10.
Unicorn/ Jeff Greenberg: 38 left.
Uniphoto: 30.
Westlight: 93; Bill Lisenby: 20–21 statue.

General Consultant
Rev. Joseph A. Komonchak, Ph.D.

Official Theological Consultant
Most Rev. Edward K. Braxton, Ph.D., S.T.D.
Auxiliary Bishop of St. Louis

Publisher
Gerard F. Baumbach, Ed.D.

Editor in Chief
Moya Gullage

Pastoral Consultant
Rev. Msgr. John F. Barry

Scriptural Consultant
Rev. Donald Senior, C.P., Ph.D., S.T.D.

General Editors
Norman F. Josaitis, S.T.D.
Rev. Michael J. Lanning, O.F.M.

Catechetical and Liturgical Consultants
Eleanor Ann Brownell, D. Min.
Joseph F. Sweeney
Helen Hemmer, I.H.M.
Mary Frances Hession
Maureen Sullivan, O.P., Ph.D.
Don Boyd

"The Ad Hoc Committee to Oversee the Use of the Catechism,
National Conference of Catholic Bishops,
has found this catechetical text to be in conformity
with the *Catechism of the Catholic Church*."

Nihil Obstat
✠ Most Reverend George O. Wirz
Censor Librorum

Imprimatur
✠ Most Reverend William H. Bullock
Bishop of Madison
July 21, 1997

The *Nihil Obstat* and *Imprimatur* are official
declarations that a book or pamphlet is free of
doctrinal or moral error. No implication is contained
therein that those who have granted the *Nihil Obstat*
and *Imprimatur* agree with the contents, opinions, or
statements expressed.

Printed in the United States of America.

S is a registered trademark of William H. Sadlier, Inc.

Home Office:
9 Pine Street
New York, NY 10005–1002

ISBN: 0–8215-5653-3
89/03

A Course on Catholic Belief

Part II: The Church and the Holy Spirit

The Amazing Search Goes On

Introduction to Creed Part II

WE are about to continue an exciting exploration of our Catholic beliefs. Before we do, we should recall some of the important things we have already learned. Chief among these things is what we learned about faith. Faith is a gift and a grace. Faith enables us to begin to know God as God knows himself. That is why faith is a virtue. It gives us power. Faith gives us the power to go beyond our human understanding and beyond what we can see and feel and touch around us. We cannot do this on our own. Faith empowers us to see through the "eyes of God." It was because of faith that this book was written for you.

As people of faith, we look to all that God has revealed to us. God has opened himself to us and has let us know his deepest Self. Understanding divine revelation is essential to our whole life of faith. In fact it is the basis of everything Christians believe, and it helps to identify who we are as Catholics. The most important things we know about God come from one source: God himself. Through revelation God tells us not only about himself but also about ourselves.

Now we are ready to begin the second part of our exploration. We will continue our study of Jesus and his teachings. We will also look in depth at the Church and what it means to be a member of the Church. If we really understand all that is here, we will be informed Catholics, excited about the mysteries of God and ready to take on the challenge of bringing the world to Christ.

Let's begin.

THE GOOD NEWS OF JESUS CHRIST

C H A P T E R 1

Great and wonderful are your works,
Lord God almighty.

Revelation 15:3

WHAT difference does Jesus' resurrection from the dead make in people's lives? Is it really that important in your life?

The Paschal Mystery

If Jesus had not risen from the dead, we might never have heard of him, and Christianity would not exist. Jesus' life would have been a failure and would have ended in defeat. There would not be much good news to share, and no one would have wanted to write a New Testament.

But Jesus did rise from the dead. The testimony of his followers and of believers from the beginning has been absolutely clear. Soon after his death on the cross and his burial, they began to experience his presence in a whole new way. The gospels do not describe his resurrection but speak of finding the empty tomb. According to Paul's account in 1 Corinthians 15:3–8, Jesus appeared to more than five hundred of his disciples.

Was it easy for all the followers of Jesus to believe that he had risen? Eyewitness accounts in the gospels relate that it was difficult for some. When the apostle Thomas, for example, heard the testimony of others to the resurrection, he did not believe it at first. When he heard that others had seen the Lord, Thomas said, "Unless I see the mark of the nails in his hands and put my finger into the nailmarks and put my hand into his side, I will not believe." Then a week later, when the risen Christ appeared to the disciples, he said to Thomas, "Put your finger here and see my hands, and bring your hand and put it into my side, and do not be unbelieving, but believe." Thomas's response was "My Lord and my God!" (John 20:25, 27–28). It took a lot to get Thomas to believe!

Jesus said to Thomas, "Have you come to believe because you have seen me? Blessed are those who have not seen and have believed" (John 20:29). At that moment Jesus was calling each of us who believe in him "blessed." What does that mean to you?

The resurrection of Jesus was a unique event, of course. Nothing like it had ever happened before. It astonished the followers of Jesus and challenged everything that they knew. In the resurrection of Jesus, God had brought to completion the salvation of the world and all that he wanted to accomplish in Christ. Jesus' crucifixion was not his final moment. It was in the resurrection that he was victorious over sin and death.

After a short time the appearances of the risen Christ came to an end, for Christ had to return to his Father. We call Christ's return to the Father his *ascension*. Jesus, risen from the dead, had entered into a whole new life, one that could not be limited to an earthly existence. That is why the gospel writer said that Jesus "parted from them and was taken up to heaven" (Luke 24:51).

With the ascension Jesus Christ was exalted in glory and enthroned at the right hand of the Father (Acts 2:33–35). There Jesus is our high priest, the one mediator between God and humanity (1 Timothy 2:5). This means that Jesus Christ offers all our prayers to the Father. This is why we pray at Mass, "Through him, with him, in him, in the unity of the Holy Spirit, all glory and honor is yours, almighty Father, for ever and ever. Amen."

For us the resurrection and ascension of Christ are not simply distant memories. We share in the new life of Christ right now. Just as we were once dead in sin, now we rise with Christ in Baptism to newness of life. This is our sharing in the death and resurrection of Jesus Christ, our paschal lamb, and the salvation he won for us.

Some people have spent a lifetime trying to summarize the wondrous events of Jesus' life, his teaching, and all that he did for us out of love. But we can summarize it all in one simple phrase: the paschal mystery. The *paschal mystery* refers to the passion, death, resurrection, and ascension of Christ. These are the most important events in our redemption. Through these events Jesus Christ brought salvation to the whole world.

In your journal write a letter to the risen Christ. Tell him what is happening in your life. Tell him what he means to you.

The Truth of the Gospels

Because of the resurrection Christians see the world in a whole new way. Just as a lamp lights up a dark room, so our belief in the resurrection enables us to see Jesus more clearly and to understand his message. This was the experience of Jesus' first followers and of the early Church community. That is why the gospels and the rest of the New Testament were written: to celebrate the paschal mystery and to share the good news of Christ in the light of the resurrection.

Some people, however, may have doubts about the truth of the gospels. They feel that the New Testament accounts are incredible, that they cannot be believed or trusted. They wonder how Jesus could have done the things that he did.

Even for nonbelievers there are certain things about the New Testament that cannot be denied. The first has to do with the closest followers of Jesus, the twelve apostles. As fishermen they had to be strong, rough, and ready. They were full of life and knew what hard work was. It would have been unlikely for such no-nonsense individuals to have been fooled easily. Only someone powerful in word and deed could have attracted the apostles, convincing them to follow him and give up everything.

Jesus was just that type of individual. When he asked the apostles to follow him, they left everything and went everywhere with him. However, when Jesus was condemned to death by crucifixion, the apostles were afraid that they would suffer the same fate. All but one deserted Jesus for fear of their lives. They went and hid.

Only one thing transformed this fearful band: the resurrection. When they recognized the risen Lord and knew that he was still among them, they were filled with excitement. Transformed by the power of the Holy Spirit, they went out and boldly proclaimed the good news of Jesus. They did this with a unanimous voice. Remember that these were simple fishermen, not educated or used to public speaking. How could they have changed so quickly if the risen Christ were not with them?

Moreover the message that they shared was an unpopular one. Suddenly, after the resurrection, they as Jews were preaching a message that all Jews would find blasphemous: that a man should be worshiped as God. Their message was one that the rest of the world would say made no sense. Would anyone want to believe in a savior who had to die? Was it sensible to believe that a small-town carpenter from the middle of nowhere was now Lord of the universe? Yet this is exactly what the early Church preached.

How can we be sure that the gospel picture of Jesus is really true? What would you say?

Scripture UPDATE

Mary Magdalene is the only person to appear in all four gospel accounts as a primary witness to Christ's resurrection. Her testimony was crucial to the early Church. This is an amazing fact when we consider that at the time of Jesus a woman's testimony was not legally acceptable. It was accepted only when verified by the testimony of men. This acceptance of Mary Magdalene is another surprising turn of events in the gospels.

Filled with Surprises

For people of the first century and for us, too, each page of the gospels is filled with surprises. Who would have imagined that the Son of God would appear on earth as a poor, unknown Nazarene, yet filled with love, gentleness, and the best of human qualities? Who would have thought that the Savior of the world would spend his time with sinners and lepers and all the outcasts of society? Who would have thought that the Messiah would criticize those in power and yet find time for those who had no power, especially women and children? No one could have thought up a religious leader like Jesus, least of all the apostles.

Not only that, but the first followers of Jesus were hated for their message. The early Church was even outlawed in the Roman Empire. At first it had to be an underground Church willing to suffer persecution and martyrdom. Belief in Jesus could send people to the Roman Coliseum, where they would be fed to lions.

The early Christians gained nothing of material importance because of their faith in the risen Christ. They did not become wealthy or powerful. Saint Paul said, "I even consider everything as a loss because of the supreme good of knowing Christ Jesus my Lord. For his sake I have accepted the loss of all things and I consider them so much rubbish, that I may gain Christ and be found in him" (Philippians 3:8–9). No one could say these words without being sure of the truth. People have trusted in the truth of the New Testament for almost two thousand years. It is the truth that we, too, can experience in the risen Christ.

Is there something about Jesus that surprises you? What is it?

Why can we say the gospel message is believable? Give reasons that convince you.

Someone once said that there is a little bit of the apostle Thomas in each of us. How do you react to that statement?

OnLine WITH THE PARISH

Make a visit to your parish church. See how many signs or symbols you can find that tell you about the paschal mystery. Make a list, and share them with the group.

YOU ARE MY WITNESSES

Things to Think About

How would you explain your belief in the resurrection to someone who does not know Christ?

WORDS to REMEMBER

Find and define:

paschal mystery

_____

_____

_____

_____

CHAPTER 2

LIFE IN CHRIST

Do not let your hearts be troubled.
You have faith in God; have faith also in me.

John 14:1

THE play *The Song of the Scaffold* is set in France during the French Revolution, a time when many priests and nuns were executed. A group of Carmelite nuns are ordered by the government to abandon their religious life. They refuse and are condemned to death. They remain firm in their faith and go up to the scaffold singing. As one after another is executed, the song becomes fainter and fainter until finally there is silence.

You would think the story would end here. Instead, it has just begun. It seems that one of the nuns had been afraid; she had gone into hiding. Now she must struggle all alone with her faith, her doubts, her fears. In the end she overcomes her terror and goes to the scaffold singing.

The point of the story is that this last nun is the bravest of all. Because the fear and doubt she had to overcome were so much greater, her courage was greater, too. Her song was the sweetest. Of all Christ's teachings, which one do you think might have been the one that gave her the courage to sing that final song?

The Providence of God

Knowing that Jesus had risen from the dead changed the apostles forever. The risen Christ was with them. Now they were certain that everything Jesus had taught them was true.

At the heart of Jesus' teaching was his concern for his Father and the fulfillment of the Father's will. Jesus' entire life centered on his Father. He wanted his disciples to know that God is personally concerned for each one of us. God loves us so much, in fact, that he sent his Son to redeem us. Jesus' first recorded words in Luke's Gospel tell us of his mission: He had to be about his Father's work (Luke 2:49).

Jesus used every moment to make his Father known. If a few sparrows settled near the place where Jesus was speaking, they could be used as an example in his teaching. One day he said, "Are not five sparrows sold for two small coins? Yet not one of them has escaped the notice of God. Even the hairs of your head have all been counted. Do not be afraid. You are worth more than many sparrows" (Luke 12:6–7). How wonderful to know that God cares for each one of us so much!

We use a special term to help us remember this overwhelming love and care of God; it is God's providence. *God's providence* is his personal concern for each of his creatures. And this was Jesus' message: Trust God because God cares. Jesus tells everyone of every age about the providence of God. "Do not worry and say, 'What are we to eat?' or 'What are we to drink?' or 'What are we to wear?' All these things the pagans seek. Your heavenly Father knows that you need them all" (Matthew 6:31–32).

CATHOLIC ID

Many Catholic homes display a crucifix, a symbol of God's providence in sending us his Son as our redeemer. Do you know what the letters INRI stand for on the crucifix? According to John's Gospel an inscription was placed on the cross that read in Latin *Iesus Nazarenus Rex Iudaeorum* (meaning "Jesus of Nazareth, King of the Jews"). So the INRI on a crucifix is made up of the first letter of each word in the Latin inscription.

Providence and Prayer

Does the providence of God mean that we get anything we want at any time we want it? Does it mean that God will answer every prayer exactly the way we want? It may be that what we ask for is not good for us. For example, we might ask God to help us pass every test we take with flying colors but without studying. This would be a foolish thing to ask, since it would hurt us in our future lives. God would never want to do that.

When we place our trust in God's providence, we know that everything will work out for the best. Each of our prayers, no matter how brief, receives God's personal and undivided attention. The answer to every prayer is yes—from God's point of view. But God may not answer us exactly as we expect. And this may be hard for us to understand. When we see God face to face, we will know all the reasons for God's providence.

Can you think of a time when you thought God's answer to your prayer was no, only to find out later that it was really yes?

Sons and Daughters of God

In Jesus' teaching on the Father, there is something for everyone. For a young person who feels unloved or abandoned, Jesus has a special message: The Father cares. Our heavenly Father makes the "sun rise on the bad and the good, and causes rain to fall on the just and the unjust" (Matthew 5:45). No one is forgotten by God; no one is ever abandoned for a single instant. God's offer of forgiveness extends always to each and every one of his children. This is why Jesus could tell the story of the prodigal son (Luke 15:11–32).

In his Father's plan, Jesus tells us, there is a special place for each one of us. It is like having our own room at home where things are familiar, warm, and secure. "In my Father's house there are many dwelling places. If there were not, would I have told you that I am going to prepare a place for you? And if I go and prepare a place for you, I will come back again and take you to myself, so that where I am you also may be" (John 14:2–3).

Sometimes a person may ask, "How does God see me? Am I just one of the crowd?" It is the individual person whom God loves. Because we are one with Christ, we are truly sons and daughters of this one Father of all. That is why we can pray both individually and as a community the words Jesus taught us.

Close your eyes and quietly pray the Our Father.

The Kingdom of God

The idea of God's providence can also be seen in Jesus' teaching about the kingdom of God. According to the Gospel of Mark, Jesus opened his public ministry by proclaiming, "The kingdom of God is at hand. Repent, and believe in the gospel" (Mark 1:15). What did Jesus mean by the phrase *kingdom of God*? He used it often in his preaching and teaching but never defined it.

To understand what that sense was, we turn to the Old Testament. There we find that God is frequently referred to as king. Why did the Old Testament writers choose this word? The king was supposed to be like the father of his nation. He was to care for his people, protect them from danger, and guarantee justice, especially for the weak and oppressed. God was, therefore, their king because he took care of them.

Jesus and the people of his time were familiar with this idea of God as a king. To be part of God's kingdom meant to be loved and protected by God. The *kingdom of God* was a symbol reminding everyone that God was the Lord of the universe, who would take care of his people and bring them salvation. Members of God's kingdom would return God's love and follow God's law. God would have a central place in their lives.

The kingdom of God was not a place; it was God's rule and reign over people's lives. Jesus wanted everyone to know that they would find the kingdom of God in him. Pointing to himself he said, "Behold, the kingdom of God is among you" (Luke 17:21). Jesus was saying that the kingdom had already burst upon the world in a marvelous way through his teaching, miracles, and healing ministry. God's kingdom is found in Jesus. What a wonderful way for God to care for his people and bring us salvation.

CATHOLIC TEACHINGS

About the Kingdom

All of us must work for the coming of God's kingdom, as we pray in the Lord's Prayer. To enter God's kingdom the Church teaches that we must turn toward God and do his will. And we remember that it is God's kingdom, not ours. The final completion of the kingdom will happen as God wants.

Jesus also taught that the kingdom of God was not yet complete. It had come in a dramatic way with Jesus, but as he said, it is like a seed that was planted (Matthew 13:18–23, 31–32). The kingdom still needs to grow and be nourished by us, Jesus' disciples. We must, therefore, look to the future as we celebrate and proclaim God's saving activity in the world. We are to take an active part in making that kingdom grow, a kingdom of justice and love. That is why we pray "thy kingdom come."

Jesus was so excited about the kingdom of God that he wanted all people to know about it. So he gathered around himself a community of disciples, the Church. He did this so that we could proclaim the good news of the kingdom and work for its completion. The Church and the kingdom of God are closely connected. Catholics believe that the Church is "on earth the seed and the beginning of that kingdom" (*Catechism*, 541).

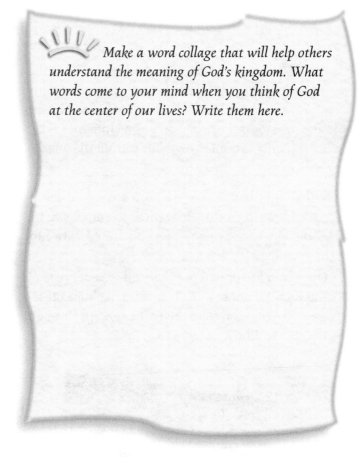

Make a word collage that will help others understand the meaning of God's kingdom. What words come to your mind when you think of God at the center of our lives? Write them here.

The Work of a Lifetime

If we want to know God, we look to Jesus. If we want to know what God asks of us, we listen to the message of Jesus. Only the risen Christ, living with us forever, can lead us to the love of God our Father. Jesus Christ is our teacher, and as he himself said, "My teaching is not my own but is from the one who sent me" (John 7:16).

On the night before he died, Jesus stressed three very important truths. He wanted to emphasize to the apostles the necessity of being united with him. These truths are:

- Only by a life united to Jesus will we ever reach the Father's house—heaven, our true home. Jesus said, "No one comes to the Father except through me" (John 14:6).

- Not only are we to be aware of our life in union with Christ, but we are also required to live it in a practical way. This we do by loving action and service on behalf of others every day. Jesus said, "This is my commandment: love one another as I love you" (John 15:12).

- Because we are united to Jesus in faith and Baptism, our lives are Christ-filled. Jesus said, "I am in my Father and you are in me and I in you" (John 14:20).

Getting to know Jesus is the work of a lifetime. We have only "scratched the surface." But that is all right. Jesus is patient. After all, he said to us, "I am with you always, until the end of the age" (Matthew 28:20).

"Getting to know Jesus is the work of a lifetime." Have you started this work? How do you plan to proceed?

If you were to explain to someone the phrase "thy kingdom come" in the Lord's Prayer, how would you go about it?

One day a friend comes to you and says, "Why should I pray? After all, to God I'm just one person among millions of others." Basing your response on the teaching of Jesus, what would you say to your friend?

One simple way to work for God's kingdom is to encourage those who have more to share with those who have less. It has been said that the coat hanging unused in your closet belongs to the one who needs it. Meet with other parish groups, and help to plan a clothing drive for those in need. Plan on ways you will assist in collecting, sorting, and delivering the clothes to local Church or civic agencies.

YOU ARE MY WITNESSES

Things to Think About

Is God a personal God to you? Do you believe he cares for you individually?

Jesus said, "No one comes to the Father except through me" (John 14:6). What do these words mean to you? How do they affect your life?

Words to REMEMBER

Find and define:

God's providence

_____

_____

_____

_____

23

CHAPTER 3

THE LORD AND GIVER OF LIFE

Come, Holy Spirit,
fill the hearts of your faithful.

WHAT do you think of when you hear the word spirit? What image comes into your mind? Does this image have anything to do with your understanding of the Holy Spirit?

Holy Spirit window, St. Peter's Basilica, Rome

Third Person of the Trinity

Sometimes called the forgotten Person of the Blessed Trinity, the Holy Spirit is the Lord and Giver of Life. Why "forgotten"? Why "Lord"? Why "Giver of Life"?

Forgotten   When you think of God, how often do you think about the Holy Spirit? Perhaps not very often. Most people probably think about God the Father or God the Son when they think of God. Even in the celebration of the liturgy, we tend to think of our prayers as addressed to God the Father through Jesus Christ our Lord. But when we do this, we forget that there is another part to the prayers of the Church: We always pray to the Father, through the Son, in the Holy Spirit.

The Holy Spirit, the third Person of the Blessed Trinity, may also be forgotten for a simple reason. It may be easier for human beings to see the Father and the Son as divine Persons. Even traditional artworks may have contributed to the problem. How many times have we seen the Holy Spirit pictured as a dove? The dove is a wonderful symbol for the Holy Spirit, of course, because it comes from the Bible itself. Nevertheless it may make it harder for some to relate to the Holy Spirit as a divine Person.

Lord   One of the titles for God with which we are most familiar is "Lord." Just think how often the title is used in the Old Testament. Rather than referring to God as *Yahweh*, the sacred name of God that was given to Moses, the Old Testament writers often used *Lord*. This was done out of reverence for God's name.

Christians know the Lord God of the Old Testament as God the Father. And because Jesus is the only Son of God, he, too, is Lord. But do Catholics usually think of the Holy Spirit as the Lord? Perhaps not often enough. Remember, the Persons of the Blessed Trinity are distinct but equal. If the Father and the Son are both Lord, the Holy Spirit must be Lord, too. *Lord* is a title that refers to divinity. Each time we recite the Nicene Creed, we recall that the Holy Spirit "is worshiped and glorified" with the Father and the Son.

Giver of Life   The Holy Spirit is the only Person of the Blessed Trinity who is called the Giver of Life. This is true for a number of reasons. Probably the most important reason is that the Holy Spirit dwells in us through sanctifying grace. This means that we share in the divine life through the power of the Holy Spirit. Saint Paul explained this truth another way. In 1 Corinthians 6:19, he reminded the early Christians that they were temples of the Holy Spirit.

There is something else important to think about. Did you know that you cannot have faith unless the Holy Spirit gives it to you? We do not usually think of faith in this way, but this is one more reason why we call the Holy Spirit the Giver of Life. The Church teaches that without the Holy Spirit we cannot have faith, we cannot believe. This Catholic truth is stated dramatically in the New Testament. There we read, "No one can say, 'Jesus is Lord,' except by the holy Spirit" (1 Corinthians 12:3).

What does this mean for our lives? Actually a great deal. Our life of faith comes to us from the Holy Spirit. The Holy Spirit, therefore, is closer to us and more important to us than most of us realize. The Holy Spirit is the Lord and Giver of Life. Knowing all this, will you think differently about the Holy Spirit from now on? Don't let the Holy Spirit remain the forgotten Person of the Blessed Trinity for you.

How can you recognize the presence of the Holy Spirit in your life?

The Holy Spirit in Scripture

Have you ever heard anyone say, "Where there is life, there is breath"? Consider the simple act of taking a deep breath. At that moment our lungs are filled with life-giving oxygen. Without breathing, we would not stay alive very long. Breath is essential to life.

The biblical writers thought about the life of the world in much the same way. They said that the "breath," or Spirit, of Yahweh was present at creation and kept it in existence. The world would be lifeless without this Spirit of God. That is why the phrase *Spirit of Yahweh* is found frequently in the Old Testament.

What did the word *spirit* mean for the biblical writers? It had a variety of meanings: breath, wind, life, soul, mind, and power. At the beginning of the Old Testament, God's work is described as a wind that "swept over the waters" at creation (Genesis 1:2) and as "the breath of life" giving life to Adam (Genesis 2:7). God is seen as acting through his Spirit.

Later in the Old Testament, the Spirit of Yahweh gave the early leaders of Israel great power and strength. In helping to form God's people, they were able to do marvelous deeds only because God's Spirit was with them. Think about Samson, who rescued God's people from their Philistine enemies. One account about this legendary strongman explained the reason for his strength. As the story goes, one day Samson was attacked by a roaring lion. "But the spirit of the LORD came upon Samson, and although he had no weapons, he tore the lion in pieces" (Judges 14:6).

Finish this sentence: The breath of the Spirit is like . . . .

28

Alive in the Spirit

In one of the best-known passages of the Bible, the prophet Ezekiel writes about an unusual vision he had. In the vision the Spirit of Yahweh leads Ezekiel to the center of a plain filled with dried human bones. Suddenly the bones begin to rattle as they come together. After they are covered with flesh, the Spirit of God enters into them. Then they come alive and stand. By sharing this vision of the bones, Ezekiel is saying that the Spirit of Yahweh gives life—and can even give life to the dead (Ezekiel 37:1–14).

Another passage in the Bible, this one from the prophet Joel in the Old Testament, helps us to discover more about the Spirit of God for our own day. Joel speaks about the future and the time of the promised Messiah. Here the Spirit of God is described as God's gift to those who act on his behalf. In this famous passage God is saying,

> Then afterward I will pour out
>   my spirit upon all mankind.
> Your sons and daughters shall prophesy,
>   your old men shall dream dreams,
>   your young men shall see visions.
> Then everyone shall be rescued
>   who calls on the name of the LORD.
> Joel 3:1, 5

In every age God's Spirit is given to those who share in God's work.

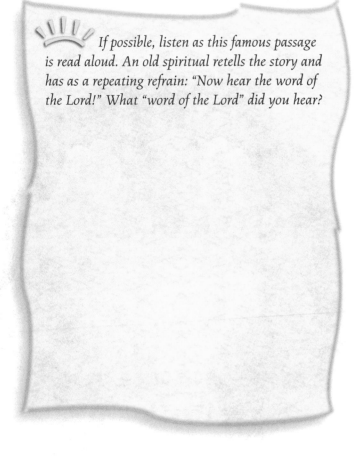

If possible, listen as this famous passage is read aloud. An old spiritual retells the story and has as a repeating refrain: "Now hear the word of the Lord!" What "word of the Lord" did you hear?

Christians know these words of Joel very well, for they appear again in the second chapter of the Acts of the Apostles. The apostle Peter quoted these words on the day of Pentecost. He tried to explain that the time of the Messiah had come, that God's work had now been brought to completion in Jesus Christ. Peter and the other disciples received the Holy Spirit because they were the followers of the risen Christ. Led by the Spirit, they would now share in Jesus' work on earth.

Do you think of yourself as someone on whom the Spirit of the Lord has been poured out? What does that mean to you? Write your thoughts in your journal.

Scripture UPDATE

Saint Paul used a rich image to describe Christians. In 1 Corinthians 6:19 he called each one of us a "temple" of the Holy Spirit. When he wrote this, Paul was thinking about the Temple of Jerusalem and how important it was in Jewish life.

Before the Temple was even built, the ark of the covenant, the symbol of God's presence with his people, was placed in a tent. A tent was used because the Israelites were nomads, wandering from place to place. Finally, after they had settled in the promised land, they constructed a permanent dwelling for the ark. This was the magnificent Temple of Jerusalem. There the ark of the covenant was placed in the holy of holies, the very heart of the Temple. This place was so sacred that the high priest alone could enter it.

The Temple was revered by all the people as the place where God dwelled among them in a special way. Knowing this, we can see what Saint Paul had in mind when he said that we are temples of the Holy Spirit. God's dwelling place is no longer to be regarded as being in one building. Now the Holy Spirit dwells in each of us. Can you imagine what the world would be like if all the followers of Jesus were to understand and appreciate what this means for their lives? It would change the world overnight!

Things to SHARE

Many Catholics are not used to referring to the Holy Spirit as Lord. How would you explain to someone that the Holy Spirit is the Lord and Giver of Life?

Explain in your own words what Saint Paul meant when he said, "No one can say, 'Jesus is Lord,' except by the holy Spirit" (1 Corinthians 12:3).

OnLine WITH THE PARISH

The Holy Spirit is calling us to build up the Church and renew the world. We are reminded of this when we pray the ancient words "Send forth your Spirit and they shall be created, and you shall renew the face of the earth."

Use these words as your prayer this week. As you pray, think of the many modern witnesses who are helping to renew the face of the earth: environmentalists, those who work for nonviolence and social justice, and those who work to end racism and sexism.

YOU ARE MY WITNESSES

Things to Think About

Name one new idea about the Holy Spirit that you learned this week. Tell why it was new for you and what it means for you today.

Why is the Holy Spirit the Giver of Life for you?

WORDS to REMEMBER

Find and define:

Holy Spirit

_____

_____

_____

_____

31

CHAPTER 4

COME HOLY SPIRIT!

Breathe on us, Breath of God,
Fill us with life anew
That we may love all that you love
And do what you would do.

Ancient Irish Prayer

If someone has fainted, we are told, "Stand back. Give him air." A drowning person is resuscitated by someone breathing air into her lungs. Mountain climbers reach heights where the air is so thin that they are disoriented and lose consciousness. We simply cannot exist without pure air. It's a biological necessity.

In 1960 Pope John XXIII looked at the Church and said, "I want to open a window and let the air in." He was talking, of course, about the fresh air of the Holy Spirit. We cannot survive without that living breath of God.

What does the Spirit, the Breath of God, do for us? In what ways does the Holy Spirit affect our lives? make us more aware? awaken us to God's presence in our lives?

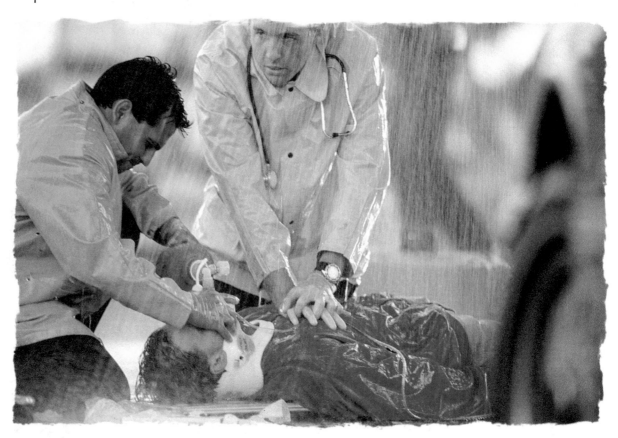

The Holy Spirit in Christ's Life

Modern Catholics may be surprised to find out how closely involved the Holy Spirit was in the life of Jesus. From the very beginning it was the Holy Spirit who came upon the Blessed Virgin Mary before Jesus' birth (Luke 1:35). Each time we recite the Nicene Creed, we profess our belief that at the incarnation the Son of God was born of the Virgin Mary "by the power of the Holy Spirit."

Later when John the Baptist baptized Jesus at the Jordan River, the Holy Spirit was present again. A dove was the sign of the Holy Spirit's presence. After Jesus' baptism the Holy Spirit drew him into the desert; there Jesus overcame the temptations of Satan. Then Jesus began his public life "in the power of the Spirit" (Luke 4:14). On returning to Nazareth, his hometown, Jesus announced the fulfillment of Isaiah's prophecy. Jesus said:

"The Spirit of the Lord is upon me,
because he has anointed me
   to bring glad tidings to the poor.
He has sent me to proclaim liberty to captives
   and recovery of sight to the blind,
      to let the oppressed go free,
and to proclaim a year acceptable to the Lord."
Luke 4:18–19

On the night before he died, Jesus promised his apostles that a new Helper would come to them. Jesus told them, "I will ask the Father, and he will give you another Advocate to be with you always, the Spirit of truth" (John 14:16–17).

To understand what Jesus is saying to us, we must know the meaning of the word *advocate*. In the New Testament the word *advocate*, or *paraclete*, has many meanings. It certainly can mean helper, but it means much more. An advocate is someone who speaks for others, who defends others and pleads for them. An advocate is also a comforter, a consoler, an intercessor, and a teacher. The Holy Spirit, then, is our intercessor, consoler, and teacher. He is the Advocate promised by the risen Lord to be with and for his disciples.

Think of the ways the Holy Spirit has been your advocate — your defender, comforter, consoler, intercessor, teacher. Write a prayer of petition or gratitude to the Holy Spirit.

The coming of the Holy Spirit was described in John's Gospel as taking place on Easter. After Jesus' death and resurrection, his apostles were afraid that they, too, would be killed. So they hid behind locked doors. John explains what happened next:

Jesus came and stood in their midst and said to them, "Peace be with you." When he had said this, he showed them his hands and his side. The disciples rejoiced when they saw the Lord. Jesus said to them again, "Peace be with you. As the Father has sent me, so I send you." And when he had said this, he breathed on them and said to them, "Receive the holy Spirit."
John 20:19–22

CATHOLIC TEACHINGS

About the Holy Spirit

How do we know the Holy Spirit, and how do we keep the Holy Spirit central in our lives? The *Catechism* (688) lists different ways. These include:

- Sacred Scripture, which was inspired by the Holy Spirit
- the tradition of the Church
- the teaching authority of the Church, which the Holy Spirit guides
- the sacraments and liturgy of the Church, in which we pray and worship together through the power of the Holy Spirit, who sanctifies us
- all our prayers, in which the Holy Spirit intercedes for us
- the lives of the saints and the ministries of the Church, in which the Holy Spirit brings us his holiness.

Pentecost

Luke's account in the Acts of the Apostles describes the coming of the Holy Spirit in a different way, a description more familiar to most people. In Acts the Holy Spirit comes upon the community of Christians in Jerusalem on the Jewish harvest feast of Pentecost (Acts 2:1–11). It was the fiftieth day after Passover, a time for the Jews to rejoice at the rich blessings God had bestowed upon Israel.

With the coming of the Holy Spirit, Pentecost would now take on new meaning for Christians. Luke said that "suddenly there came from the sky a noise like a strong driving wind." Then he said that "tongues as of fire" came to rest on each of the disciples. "They were all filled with the holy Spirit" (Acts 2:2–4).

For the first Christians this day of Pentecost was the occasion for Jesus to pour out the Holy Spirit upon them, giving them an abundance of the gifts of the Spirit. The risen Christ was sharing his life with them—and with us—in the power of the Holy Spirit. Pentecost, therefore, was the completion of Christ's passover. The coming of the Holy Spirit is the completion of the paschal mystery—all that Jesus Christ did for us.

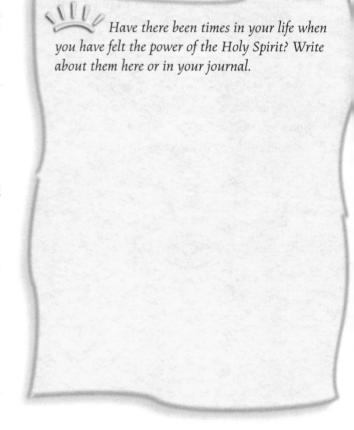

Have there been times in your life when you have felt the power of the Holy Spirit? Write about them here or in your journal.

CATHOLIC ID

One of the most recognizable stained-glass windows in the world is the window behind the main altar in Saint Peter's Basilica in the Vatican. In the window the Holy Spirit is symbolized as a dove. It reminds us of Jesus' baptism by John at the Jordan. Perhaps even more than this, it reminds us that at Baptism we are made a new creation through the power of the Holy Spirit. The biblical symbol of a dove goes all the way back to the Book of Genesis. In the story of the flood, Noah releases a dove to see whether or not the land has been renewed (Genesis 8:8–12). Thus the dove became a symbol of new life (see page 26).

Guided by the Spirit

Filled with the Holy Spirit, the early Christians went out with great excitement to bring Christ to others. These once-frightened disciples were given great power, courage, strength, and authority by the Holy Spirit. Jesus had told them, "You will receive power when the holy Spirit comes upon you, and you will be my witnesses in Jerusalem, throughout Judea and Samaria, and to the ends of the earth" (Acts 1:8).

Although the apostles had spent some of the best days of their lives with Jesus, they did not know him as fully as they thought. Jesus himself understood this. That is why Jesus said to them, "I have much more to tell you, but you cannot bear it now. But when he comes, the Spirit of truth, he will guide you to all truth" (John 16:12–13).

The coming of the Holy Spirit made a big difference in the lives of the apostles. Because Jesus sent the Holy Spirit to them, they were now ready to grasp all that he wanted them to know. Recall Jesus' words to the apostles, "The Advocate, the holy Spirit that the Father will send in my name—he will teach you everything and remind you of all that I told you" (John 14:26).

With memories refreshed and enlivened by the Holy Spirit, the apostles were able to give witness to the Jesus that they knew. The man they knew and with whom they walked was the Lord Jesus Christ, the God-Man—not dead, but alive! The Holy Spirit's coming enabled the apostles to recall and present the teachings that Jesus handed over to them for the Church throughout the ages. They now knew and understood their mission.

Today the Holy Spirit is still guiding Jesus' disciples. It is the Holy Spirit who guides the missionary activity of the Church. It is the Holy Spirit who draws so many people to the Church. It is the Holy Spirit who strengthens members of the Church to speak out against oppression, injustice, and poverty in our world.

Are you ever aware of the Holy Spirit working in the life of the Church? Give one example. Write it in your journal.

37

The Life of Grace

We are temples of the Holy Spirit. Through Baptism we have been initiated into the life of sanctifying grace, a participation in the very life of God.

Our experience of the Holy Spirit, the sanctifier, does not end with sanctifying grace, however. The Church teaches us that the Holy Spirit is active in our lives through actual graces. *Actual graces* are interventions of God in our daily lives. These interventions are urgings or promptings from the Holy Spirit. Like sparks that can ignite a fire, these graces help us to deepen our Christian life and live the good news of Jesus as members of the Church.

There are many examples of actual graces. The Holy Spirit gives them to us either directly or indirectly through other people and events in our lives. These include the good example of others or the awareness to do good that we might gain from reading a book. Actual graces might also include the feelings that come spontaneously into our lives and that help lead us to holiness.

What would happen if the Holy Spirit were no longer present? Only then might we truly understand what he means to us. Like a world without water, we could not really live without the Holy Spirit. We sometimes forget how important water is until we do not have it. Without water, green fields dry up and become deserts. Without the Holy Spirit, our spiritual lives would be much the same; they would wither away and become desertlike. The Church reminds us of this truth when we pray these words:

When you hide your face, they are lost.
   When you take away their breath, they perish
   and return to the dust from which they came.
When you send forth your breath, they are created,
   and you renew the face of the earth.
Psalm 104:29–30

Describe what the world might be like if everyone were to realize that through Baptism we become temples of the Holy Spirit.

In what ways is the Holy Spirit our advocate?

The Holy Spirit gives us actual graces to live out our Christian lives together. Very often these actual graces come to us through other people. What example can you offer to your parish family so that you might be an occasion of actual graces for others? Make sure that your example is practical and that it can be accomplished.

YOU ARE MY WITNESSES

Things to Think About

After learning so much about the Holy Spirit, do you think that you will pray in the same way as you have in the past? Why or why not?

Are you aware of actual graces that have affected your own life? What are they?

Words to Remember

Find and define:

actual graces

_____

_____

_____

_____

CHAPTER 5

THE MYSTERY OF THE CHURCH

You are fellow citizens with the holy ones
and members of the household of God,
built upon the foundation of the
apostles and prophets.

Ephesians 2:19–20

SATURDAY

evening a tornado hit with such great fury that it devastated the small town. Even the Catholic church was destroyed. The next morning Mass was celebrated in the public school gym, one of the few buildings left standing. As the people of the parish gathered together, the pastor reminded them that even though their building was gone, they were still the Church.

More Than Meets the Eye

Some people may be surprised at the pastor's words about being the Church. But he was right. The Church is more than buildings. It is really a great mystery, a mystery so deep that it is difficult to describe the Church in just a few words. That is why we are going to spend eight chapters exploring its meaning and depth.

The root meaning of the word *church* is "belonging to the Lord." In the Bible it means "a people called together." The Church is the assembly of those chosen by God in Jesus Christ, the assembly of God's people. Being the Church involves not only being the gathered community but also the process of gathering together. The Church, therefore, is not only an established group but also an event: people coming together, especially for the purpose of worshiping God and serving others. The Church is Christ's faithful people, the people of God.

The People of God

The idea of people of God goes back to Old Testament times. Israel became God's people because God chose it to be his own possession. God said, "I will take you as my own people, and you shall have me as your God" (Exodus 6:7). God's choice of this small nation to be his possession rather than other great nations took place solely from God's love. It was a grace.

Jesus, too, gathered a people to himself. The early Christian community was the new assembly of God's people. After the Pentecost experience in Jerusalem, the community gradually grew through the preaching of the apostles and their helpers. Wherever the people of God were found, they gathered together to hear God's word and to offer eucharistic worship for all that he had done for them.

Just as the choosing of Israel was the result of God's love, so, too, the Church came into being because of the love and grace of God. In fact the early Church taught that even before the creation of the world, God chose us in Christ (Ephesians 1:4) to be

"a chosen race, a royal priesthood, a holy nation, a people of his own" (1 Peter 2:9). We are a people because God dwells in us and moves among us. This means that we are a sign of God's presence in the world. God has chosen his people, and this is a mystery of divine grace.

There is also something more that we should recognize. Using the image of God's people, the writers of the New Testament saw the Church as part of the continuing story of God's dealings with his chosen people. By using the term *people of God*, they were pointing out the bond that existed between the Christian community and the people of Israel.

All this means that the early Christians did not date or place the beginning of God's people from Jesus' birth or ministry. Rather, they looked to the times of Abraham and Moses. That is why among those names that belong to God's people and were adopted by the Church, one of the most meaningful was the name *Israel*. Paul himself addressed the Christian community this way when he wrote, "Peace and mercy be . . . to the Israel of God" (Galatians 6:16).

Jesus once said, "When I am lifted up from the earth, I will draw everyone to myself" (John 12:32). He still works to draw everyone to himself through his people. Just as God once chose and gathered his people by delivering them from Egypt, now he gathers his community, the Church, through the redeeming blood of his Son. Jesus has given himself for us in order to redeem us, "to cleanse for himself a people as his own" (Titus 2:14).

The Body of Christ

The Church is people, no one of whom is perfect. Paul himself knew this when he worked with the early Christians. When we read his letters in the New Testament, we can see that he ran into many difficulties. There were disagreements among the members of the Church. Some even formed into rival groups, claiming as their authority Peter, Paul, or one of the other leaders of the Church.

Disagreements, of course, are not unusual. They go on in the Church in every age. The Church is a visible organization; and in its human reality, it is often too human. Its human weaknesses offend many and, at times, turn them away. But is the Church only a human organization?

No. The Spirit of the living God is present in the Church. The Church is founded on Jesus Christ and guided by the Holy Spirit. This is why Paul frequently mentioned that Christians are united to Christ in one common life. He taught that the Church is the body of Christ, with the life-giving Holy Spirit flowing through that body. "For in one Spirit we were all baptized into one body, whether Jews or Greeks, slaves or free persons, and we were all given to drink of one Spirit" (1 Corinthians 12:13).

Paul gave us this understanding of the Church as the body of Christ. The experience of his own conversion gave him that wise insight. One day he was on his way to the city of Damascus with one purpose in mind: to destroy the followers of Jesus. Suddenly Christ appeared to him. Paul heard a voice saying to him, "Why are you persecuting me?" When Paul asked who it was he was persecuting, the voice replied, "I am Jesus, whom you are persecuting" (Acts 9:4–5).

Paul got the message! During the rest of his lifetime, he saw more and more the connection between Jesus and his followers. Jesus Christ lives in us and we in him. Paul taught that we are one body; that is, we belong to Christ's body. Each Christian has a special role to play. Each is uniquely related to Christ. "As a body is one though it has many parts, and all the parts of the body, though many, are one body, so also Christ" (1 Corinthians 12:12).

What will you do this week to let others know that Jesus lives in you and you in him?

A Unique Image

The individual parts of a human body share a common life and cannot live apart from one another. In the same way we share the life of Christ, the head of the body that is his Church. "Now you are Christ's body, and individually parts of it" (1 Corinthians 12:27). Individually and together we are the fullness of Christ, the whole Christ. If others want to meet Christ now in our time, they meet him in us! What a wonderful way to think of Jesus Christ and his Church.

Paul was not alone in his thinking. His image of the Church as the body of Christ is similar to other New Testament images, such as the image of the vine and branches (John 15:1–8). These comparisons try to express the close connection between Jesus Christ and his people. They also bring out the closeness that Church members must have with one another. After all, we are members of the same body. The Church in the New Testament, then, is most appropriately called the body of Christ. But the image does not replace that of the people of God—it deepens it. The Church is the people of God as the body of Christ.

It is clear, then, that *body of Christ* is a unique image. It expresses a relation between Christ and the Church that is as close as can be imagined. It reminds us that Christ and the Church are so close that no one can come to Christ without the Church. Our personal union with Christ, therefore, also involves our belonging to the Church. This means that no one can be an isolated follower of Jesus Christ; one must be a member of the Church.

The chart on the following page lists some familiar images of the Church. Study them and discuss their meaning for your life.

Other New Testament Images of the Church

Image	Biblical Source	Meaning
ark of salvation	1 Peter 3:19–22	The Church is compared to Noah's ark. As a means of salvation through water, the ark reminds us of Baptism and our initiation into the Church.
bride of Christ	1 Corinthians 11:2	The union of Christ and his members is one of intimate, mutual, and permanent interdependence.
building on a rock	Matthew 16:18–19	*Rock* is a title of God in the Old Testament. The Church teaches and guides us with God's authority.
mother	Revelation 12:17	Through the sacraments the Church brings us into and nourishes us in the divine life.

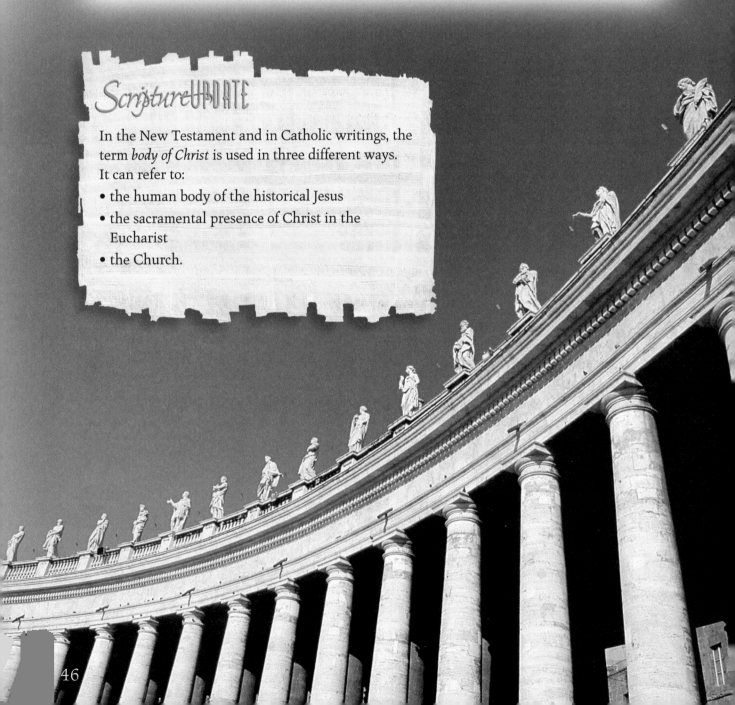

Scripture UPDATE

In the New Testament and in Catholic writings, the term *body of Christ* is used in three different ways. It can refer to:

• the human body of the historical Jesus

• the sacramental presence of Christ in the Eucharist

• the Church.

Things to SHARE

Choose your favorite image of the Church and explain it.

What experience led Saint Paul to his understanding of the Church as the body of Christ?

OnLine WITH THE PARISH

What have you done lately for your parish community? You share together the same life in Christ. How do you show it? Talk with your group and with your catechist. Choose one way you will offer to be of service in your parish.

YOU ARE MY WITNESSES

Things to Think About

Why is the Church called the people of God?

Have you ever thought of yourself as "belonging to the Lord"? What does it mean for you to be chosen by God to be part of his people? How do you show it?

WORDS to REMEMBER

Find and define:

body of Christ

_____

_____

_____

_____

A Community Unlike Any Other

Come to him, a living stone, . . .
and, like living stones, let yourselves
be built into a spiritual house.

1 Peter 2:4, 5

LIKE living stones . . . .

Isn't it interesting that the practical, down-to-earth fisherman would choose such a poetic image to tell us about the Church? We must come to Christ the cornerstone, Peter tells us, and like living stones be built on him into a "spiritual house."

Do you feel that you are a "living" part of the Church? Or do you see yourself out on the rock pile — unused, unwilling, and unavailable for service?

Human and Divine

It is clear that the Church is an organized community unlike any other. As the people of God, it is a union of people guided by the Holy Spirit and under the direction of its leaders. Like any other group of people, it is both shaped by and shapes history. It rejoices in the goodness of its members but suffers from their weaknesses, too.

As the body of Christ, the Church is made up of both human and divine dimensions. It is presided over by human beings, yet they act with the authority they have received from God (Matthew 18:18). When the Church proclaims God's word in human language, it relies, not on human wisdom, but on the power of the Holy Spirit (1 Corinthians 2:13).

Whenever the members of the Church worship together, they are more than an ordinary group of people; they are a people intimately united with their Lord (1 Corinthians 11:27). When they have sinned and they repent, mere human words spoken by a priest become the bearers of divine forgiveness (John 20:23).

We can say that the Church combines what is human and divine, what is earthly and heavenly, and what is found in time and in eternity. Like the moon reflecting the light of the sun, the Church brings the light of Christ to the world. It is clear, then, that the Church is a mystery, a truth of faith that we know only because God revealed it to us.

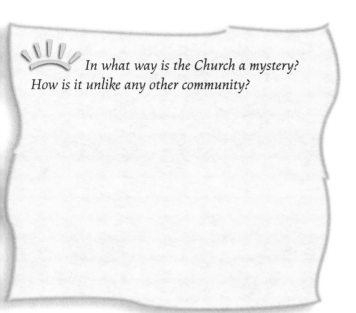

In what way is the Church a mystery? How is it unlike any other community?

The Family of God

The Church is a mystery and the union of what is human and divine. We probably do not think of it that way each day, but we should. We can also think of the Church as our family, the family of God. This idea goes back to the earliest times when the Church was spoken of as "the household of God," another way of saying God's family (1 Peter 4:17). We enter this family through Baptism, the sacrament by which we become children of God.

It is in the parish, the basic unit of the Church, that most Catholics live out their membership in the family of God. All the members begin to share a common, or family, life through the sacraments of Baptism, Confirmation, and Eucharist. And these sacraments of initiation, as well as the other sacraments, are celebrated in the parish.

The members of the Church, like the members of any family, are all different. Each has his or her own gifts and talents and graces. Each fills a different role. Some are ordained deacons. Others are ordained priests. Still others are ordained bishops, who share the fullness of the priesthood. Bishops, priests, and deacons are called the clergy. The *clergy* are the members of the Church who have received the sacrament of Holy Orders. Most members of the Church, however,

are the laity. The *laity* are the baptized members of the Church. This includes everyone who is not in Holy Orders or who is not a vowed *religious*, a member of a religious order or community. No less than the clergy and religious, the laity have an important part in the whole life of the family of God.

Clergy, religious, and laity depend on one another in the parish family and must work as a team. Paul wrote about the different activities of various members of the Church family. He explained that the smooth functioning of the body depends on the cooperation of all its parts. You may wish to read what he has to say about this in 1 Corinthians 12:18–26.

Among laity, religious, and clergy there must be a deep bond. Each works to bring the risen Christ into the world. Each is able to do this in ways that the other cannot. Each is able to do for people what the other cannot do. Together they complete one another in the sense of being united in Christ for the common good of everyone they meet.

 **CATHOLIC ID** One way the laity are actively involved in the life of a parish is through the parish council. A *parish council* is a group of parishioners who are elected or appointed to help the pastor in the administration of the parish. The pastor presides over the council, and council members work closely with him. They advise him about the needs of the parish, including parish finances, education, liturgy, and social justice.

From your experience as a member of a parish, complete the chart on the following page by describing the different functions of parish members.

Who's Who in the Parish	
Name	Your Description
pastor	
other priests	
deacons	
pastoral ministers	
eucharistic ministers	
lectors	
altar servers	
ushers	
director of religious education	
Catholic school principal	
religious sisters	
religious brothers	
catechists	
teachers	
director of music	
members of parish organizations	

Essential Features

What makes you the person you are? Is it the color of your hair or the fact that you wear glasses? Of course not. Things like these are only superficial, only on the surface. Each of us is so much more. Each of us is unique and has a set of unique characteristics. Without your own unique characteristics, you would not be who you are.

The same is true of the Church. The Church also has certain characteristics, or essential features. Without them the Church would not be the Church that Jesus founded. Four essential features of the Church are that it is one, holy, catholic, and apostolic. These characteristics are so important for Catholics that we profess our belief about them each week at Mass. Let's look at them more closely.

Unity: A Gift Never to Be Lost   When we say that the Church is *one*, we are talking about the unity of the Church. And this unity of the Church comes from its source, the Blessed Trinity. This means that God the Father calls us into the one body of Christ, to whom we belong. The Holy Spirit gives life to that body.

From the earliest times this wonderful unity of the Church has been expressed in its one profession of faith handed on to each generation from the time of the apostles. The unity of the Church is also expressed in the celebration of divine worship, especially the sacraments. We are united in one Baptism and gather as one around the table of the Lord in the Eucharist. Through the sacrament of

Holy Orders, the Church can trace its unity back to the time of the apostles. Paul described this unity when he wrote, "Because the loaf of bread is one, we, though many, are one body, for we all partake of the one loaf" (1 Corinthians 10:17). We are one in the Lord and constantly striving for greater unity.

A Work of Grace　The Church is *holy* because our sins are forgiven, and we are sanctified, or made holy, by our union with Christ. Through our Baptism in Christ's death and resurrection, we enter into the life of grace, which is God's own life. God alone is holy, and we participate in that holiness through the Church, especially the sacraments.

Christ so loved the Church that he sent us the Holy Spirit. The Holy Spirit fills and guides the Church for all time. The Church teaches us that as members of the Church we are temples of the Holy Spirit. Through Jesus Christ the whole structure of the Church is held together and "grows into a temple sacred in the Lord"; in Christ we also "are being built together into a dwelling place of God in the Spirit" (Ephesians 2:21–22).

As members of the Church, we are also bearers of the fruits of the Holy Spirit: love, joy, peace, patience, kindness, generosity, faithfulness, gentleness, self-control (Galatians 5:22). As baptized members of the Church, we are a holy people and constantly striving for greater holiness.

At Home Around the World　The Church is *catholic* because it is universal and missionary. It is meant for the whole world and has a message for the whole world. The Church can never be narrow or associate itself with only one place or time. Jesus never placed any limits on the Church, where it was to go or thrive. Rather, the Church must gather to itself all who are called by God.

The Church, therefore, is not called catholic because it does missionary work. Rather, the Church engages in missionary activity precisely because it is catholic and has a message for all. That is why Jesus says, "Go, therefore, and make disciples of all nations" (Matthew 28:19). The Church is catholic and must never rest from bringing Christ to the world. The task is not over until the end of time.

> *Because you belong to a Church that is catholic, you must be open to all. What impact does this have on any prejudices you might have?*

Group of teens praying together during World Youth Day

The True Foundation   The Church is *apostolic* because it was founded on Christ and the apostles. Jesus chose the apostles to lead the early Church in his name. They were sent by Christ himself—by him and by no other—to be his witnesses "to the ends of the earth" (Acts 1:8). Guided by the Holy Spirit, the apostles handed on the teachings of Christ. That is why the Church always looks back to the apostolic foundation of Peter and the other apostles when it looks for the deposit of faith. This apostolic foundation can never be replaced.

Until Christ comes again at the end of time, the Church will continue in the apostolic tradition under the leadership of the pope and bishops, the successors to the apostles. They teach, sanctify, and govern the Church in the name of Christ. The Church is apostolic and must always strive to stay in tune with its true apostolic foundation.

CATHOLIC TEACHINGS

About the Church's Essential Features

It is Christ, through the Holy Spirit, who makes the Church one, holy, catholic, and apostolic. And it is Christ who calls the Church "to realize each of these qualities" (*Catechism*, 811).

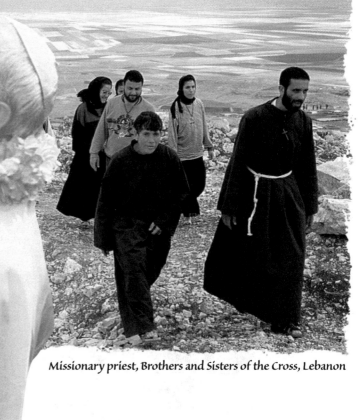

Missionary priest, Brothers and Sisters of the Cross, Lebanon

54

Pope John Paul II in Ghana, Africa

Should people give up on the Church when they hear about or meet Church members — clergy, religious, or laity — who are weak or make mistakes? Discuss responses.

Share your ideas on what it means for the Church to be both human and divine.

No one in a parish can be just a spectator. That goes for the youngest member as well as the oldest. That is because each member is a member of the body of Christ. Using the chart "Who's Who in the Parish," brainstorm creative ways young people can take an active part in the parish as members of the household of God.

YOU ARE MY WITNESSES

You invite a friend to go to Mass with you one Sunday. Your friend says to you, "I don't need the Church. I follow Christ in my own way, and that is just as good." Your response?

Tell in your own words why the Church is a mystery of faith.

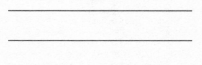

Find and define:

catholic

_____

_____

_____

_____

CHAPTER 1

A STRONG
FOUNDATION

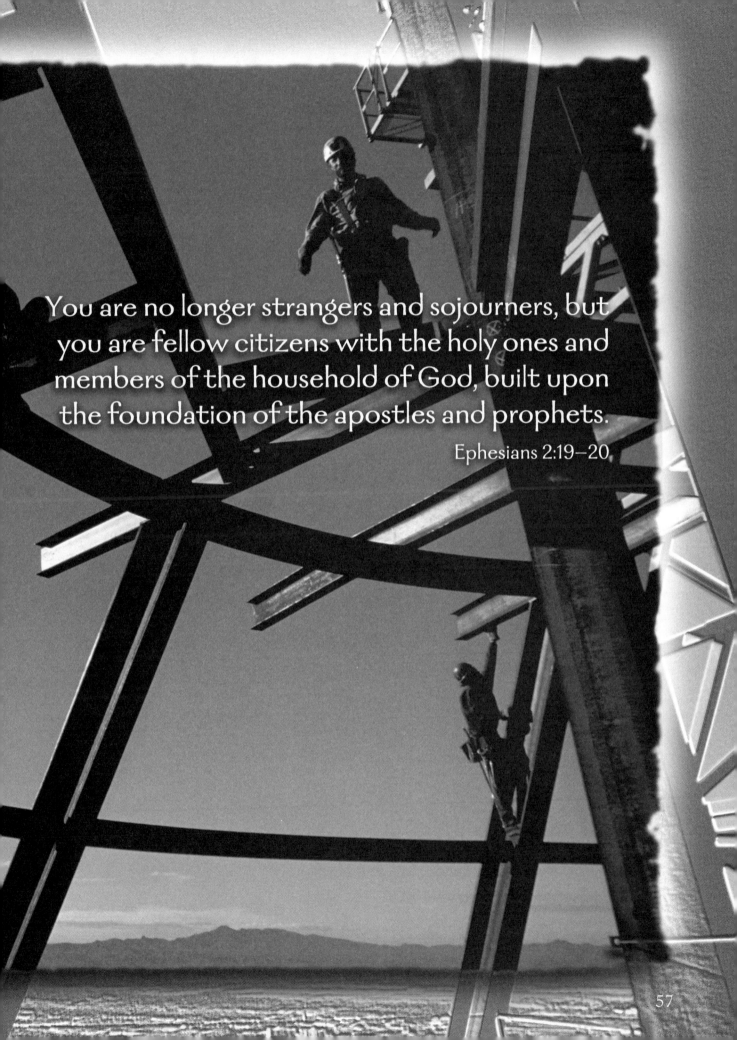

You are no longer strangers and sojourners, but you are fellow citizens with the holy ones and members of the household of God, built upon the foundation of the apostles and prophets.

Ephesians 2:19–20

If the Church is founded on Christ and the apostles, what happened after the apostles died? Where did the people of God turn for leadership? What do you think?

58

From Apostle to Bishop

The roots of Church leadership extend back to Jesus and the apostles. Jesus handpicked a group we know as the Twelve and gathered them around himself. These were the apostles. From their close contact with Jesus, they were privileged to know "the mysteries of the kingdom of heaven" (Matthew 13:11). Jesus shared his mission and authority with them. They were to be the pillars upon which he would build his Church.

While Jesus was speaking to the Twelve one day, he asked them what people were saying about him and who he was. It was Simon Peter who finally spoke up and said, "You are the Messiah, the Son of the living God" (Matthew 16:16). Simon was speaking for the other apostles as well when he said that Jesus was the promised Messiah.

Jesus answered this expression of faith in him by changing Simon's name to Peter, meaning "rock." Jesus said, "I say to you, you are Peter, and upon this rock I will build my church, and the gates of the netherworld shall not prevail against it. I will give you the keys to the kingdom of heaven" (Matthew 16:18–19).

Jesus' special recognition of Peter gave him a place of authority above the others but not apart from them. The work of teaching, governing, and sanctifying people in Jesus' name was not to be his alone. It was to be shared by all the apostles with Peter. The Twelve formed a single body, or college; they received their mission together. Although the keys to the kingdom were given to Peter's care, he and the other apostles were the foundation of that Church in which Christ is the cornerstone.

After the ascension of Jesus and Pentecost, the apostles traveled to every part of the world that they knew. With great courage they followed the promptings of the Holy Spirit and established local Churches wherever they went. They did not stay in any one place, however, because they were leaders of the whole Church.

A Wider Ministry   The twelve apostles shared their work with others in the wider ministry of founding and organizing Churches. Sometimes these others, like Paul, were also called "apostles" even though they were not part of the original Twelve. But other names, such as "prophet" and "evangelist," were also used to describe these apostolic leaders. The reason is that official titles had not yet been determined by the Church.

A Local Ministry   Once a local Church became established, the apostolic leaders moved on. But they chose and left behind local Church officers, whom they had ordained by the laying on of hands. These men, too, were called by a number of different titles: "pastor" or "teacher" or "presbyter" (priest, elder) or "bishop" (overseer). The words seemed to have been used interchangeably. Assisted by deacons, these local Church officers presided over their Churches under the authority of the apostles, prophets, and evangelists. But their official titles, like those of the apostolic leaders, had not yet been determined.

The Threefold Ministry   After the Church began to spread around the world, the general traveling ministry of the apostolic leaders became less necessary. It gradually died out as the apostolic leaders passed away. Some of them may have settled in local Churches, as we know James had done in Jerusalem and Timothy in Ephesus. In any event the title of bishop became reserved only for the successors of the apostolic leaders and the title of presbyter (priest) for the other local officers. The title of deacon remained unchanged.

The ministry of the apostles, therefore, was continued and assured in the ministry of the local bishops. These bishops were the vital link to the apostles and thus to Christ himself. By A.D. 110 Ignatius of Antioch could speak of the threefold ministry of bishop, presbyter (priest), and deacon as "established in the farthest parts of the earth." Through the laying on of hands, we have the same threefold ministry today.

If you could ask a question of an early Church leader who knew Jesus, what would the question be?

Acting in the Name of Christ

Imagine that you are a member of the early Church and that it is a time of persecution. During the Eucharist one Sunday, a letter is read to the assembled community. The letter is from the bishop of a neighboring Church. His name is Ignatius, the bishop of Antioch, and not many days ago he was led away in chains. Knowing that you and other Christians might be afraid, Ignatius wants you to be strong in your faith and to know what is important. This is what he writes:

> All of you must follow your bishop, as Jesus followed the Father, and follow the presbyters as you would the apostles; and to the deacons pay respect, as to God's law. Let no one carry on the work of the Church apart from the bishop. There is only one true Eucharist: the one over which the bishop or one of his delegates presides. Wherever the bishop is, that is where the people should be; even as where Jesus is, there is the Universal Church.
> *Letter to the Smyrnaeans,* 8

What a clear picture Ignatius presents of the Church. The people of God are assembled at the altar, with the bishop or one of his presbyters presiding over the celebration of the Eucharist. The bishop stands at the center of the community. Assisted by the presbyters and deacons, he leads the Church with the authority of the apostles and in the name of Jesus. In fact he is the vital link to them in the life of the Church.

How important is the bishop? Very important! Without him there would be no presbyters (priests) or deacons because they are ordained by the bishop. This means that there could be no Eucharist and that most of the other sacraments could not be celebrated. Without the bishop the link to Christ through the apostles would be missing. That is why Cyprian, a third-century Father of the Church, could say, "The bishop is in the Church and the Church in the bishop."

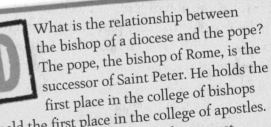

CATHOLIC ID

What is the relationship between the bishop of a diocese and the pope? The pope, the bishop of Rome, is the successor of Saint Peter. He holds the first place in the college of bishops as Peter held the first place in the college of apostles. Therefore the pope and the other bishops must always work together. One bishop does not work independently of the others.

Teaching, Governing, Sanctifying

Jesus wanted all his disciples to be servants of one another, not masters. He said, "Let the greatest among you be as the youngest, and the leader as the servant," and "I am among you as the one who serves" (Luke 22:26, 27). This does not mean, however, that no one was to have authority in the Church. Every human organization must have some authority to help it identify itself, to help bring unity, and to resolve any conflicts or problems. The Church is no different.

Jesus is the source of all authority and ministry in the Church. Knowing how important this authority would be, he shared it with the apostles and those who were to succeed them. That is why bishops succeed the apostles in their office of teaching, governing, and sanctifying in the name of Christ.

Teaching The bishops are the chief teachers of the Church. As the chief teachers, they succeed to the office of the apostles and prophets. As links to the apostles, the bishops are charged with the sacred duty of passing on the complete and authentic teaching of Jesus and the apostolic Church. Guided by the Holy Spirit, they are to transmit and make clear what has been revealed to us by God; they are entrusted by God to safeguard the great deposit of faith that belongs to the Church.

What do these pictures tell us about the work of a bishop?

This work of the bishops is done as a service to the other members of the Church so that our faith may rest secure on a strong foundation.

Governing   The bishops are the chief authorities and pastors (shepherds) in the Church. Each bishop exercises authority in his diocese. He also shares a worldwide authority with the pope and the other bishops. In the diocese the bishop directs the life of the Church. He is the visible sign of its unity. He coordinates its work, he helps it to keep focused on its true mission of building God's kingdom, and he brings people of different backgrounds together in harmony. Like Christ the Good Shepherd, the bishop is to watch over all those under his care, especially the weak.

Sanctifying   The bishop has the fullness of the sacrament of Holy Orders. He is the chief priest of the diocese and shares this priesthood with the presbyters, whom he ordains. With these coworkers he sanctifies the Church through prayer and the ministry of both word and sacrament, especially the Eucharist. Through the bishop we are reminded that the Eucharist is the center of the life of the Church.

Do you think the person who has the most authority should be the one who serves others? Why or why not? What did Jesus think?

What is meant by the threefold ministry?

Do you think leadership is necessary in the Church? Explain.

At every Mass you will hear the bishop of your diocese mentioned by his first name. Listen closely. The next time you hear your bishop's name at Mass, remember how challenging his ministry is, and pray for him.

YOU ARE MY WITNESSES

Things to Think About

What does it mean for you to know that our bishops are the Church's links to the apostles and to Christ himself?

Why should we, as Catholics, listen to our bishops when they speak about issues that affect us today?

WORDS to REMEMBER

Find and define:

presbyter

_____

_____

_____

_____

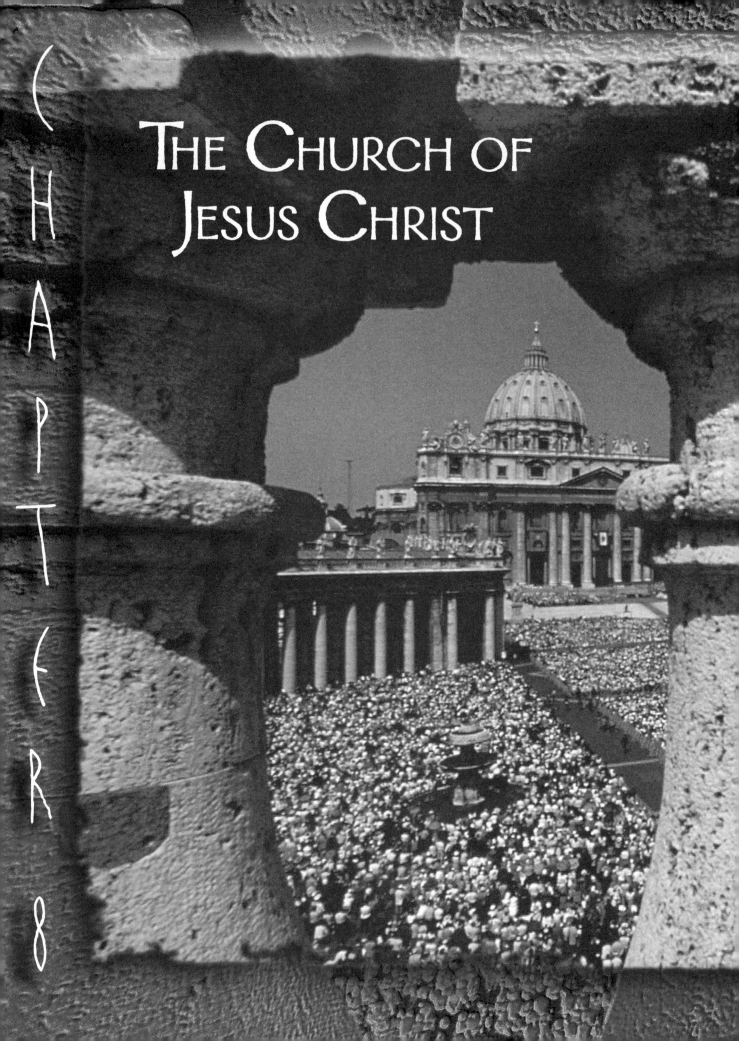

THE CHURCH OF JESUS CHRIST

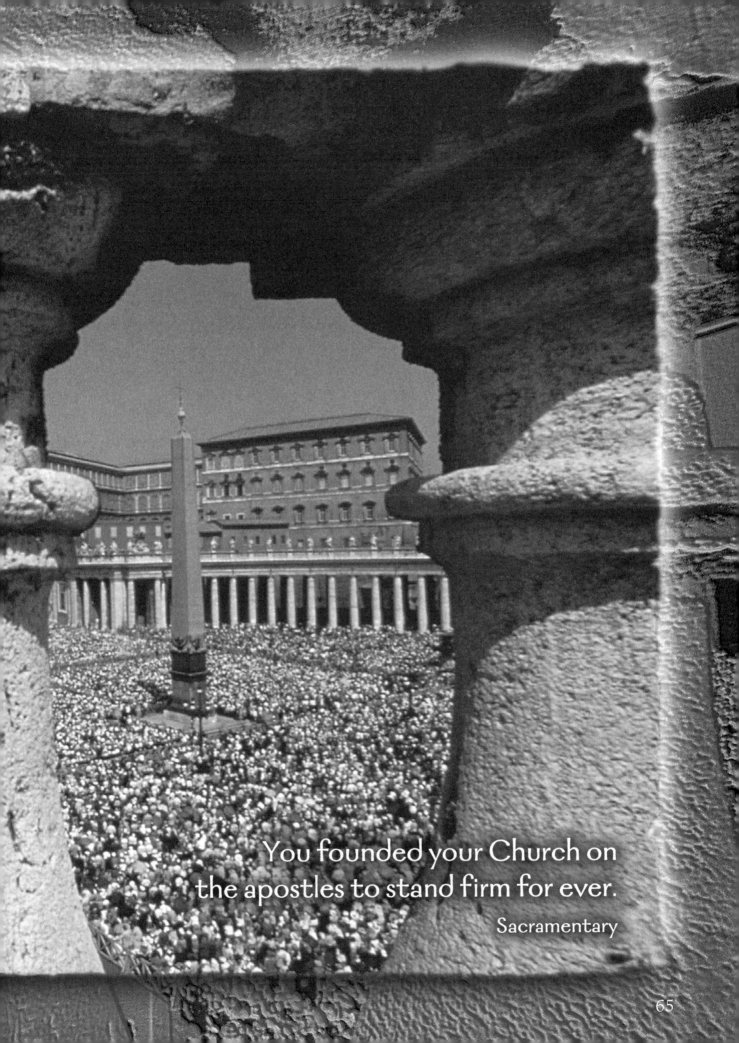

CHAPTER 8

You founded your Church on
the apostles to stand firm for ever.

Sacramentary

RECENTLY some young Americans found themselves in St. Peter's square in Rome. They joined thousands who had gathered for a Mass with the Holy Father.

"It was like swimming in a sea of people from all over the world, speaking every language imaginable!" one of them remarked later.

"Then Mass began," said another. "It was amazing. Suddenly nationalities and languages didn't seem to matter. We were all one. I'll never forget it."

Have you ever had an experience like this? What does it really mean to belong to the people of God?

The Church of Christ

A correct understanding of the Church is so important for Catholics that it was one of the major topics of the Second Vatican Council. After long reflection and discussion, the bishops, who had gathered from every part of the world, gave us a deep insight into the meaning of the Church. They taught that the Church of Christ, the Church founded upon Christ and the apostles, is made up of a number of "elements." Without these basic elements there would be no Church.

First and foremost the Church is one, holy, catholic, and apostolic. These characteristics

are essential features of the Church. But there are other elements that are essential to the Church, too. These include both visible and invisible elements.

The *visible elements*, as the name suggests, are those that make the Church a recognizable body in the world. After all, the Church is an organization of people with leaders, beliefs, laws, and practices. This organization can be readily seen and recognized by all. Among the vital elements of the Church that make it visible, the council bishops mentioned the following:

- Scripture, which is the Church's written record of God's revelation. Scripture cannot be changed or ignored because it is a permanent document.
- Baptism, along with the other sacraments of the Church. Remember that no one can become a member of the Church without first having been baptized.
- Episcopacy, which is the office of bishop. This includes the pope, the bishop of Rome. Episcopacy links the Church through the apostles to Christ himself.
- Eucharist, which is the source and high point of the Church's life.
- Doctrines of faith, which are the teachings that come down to us from the time of the apostles.
- Devotion to Mary, the Mother of God. Her spiritual motherhood extends to all the members of the Church.

Second Vatican Council, 1962–1965

The *invisible elements* have to do with the Church's inner life. As the name suggests, the elements cannot be seen except in their results. The members of the Church show these elements by the way they live. Among the vital elements of the Church that cannot be seen, the council bishops mentioned the following:

- The life of grace, which is a participation in the very life of God.
- The theological virtues of faith, hope, and love, which are gifts from God. They are powers enabling us to act as children of God.
- The gifts of the Holy Spirit, who is continually sanctifying the Church.

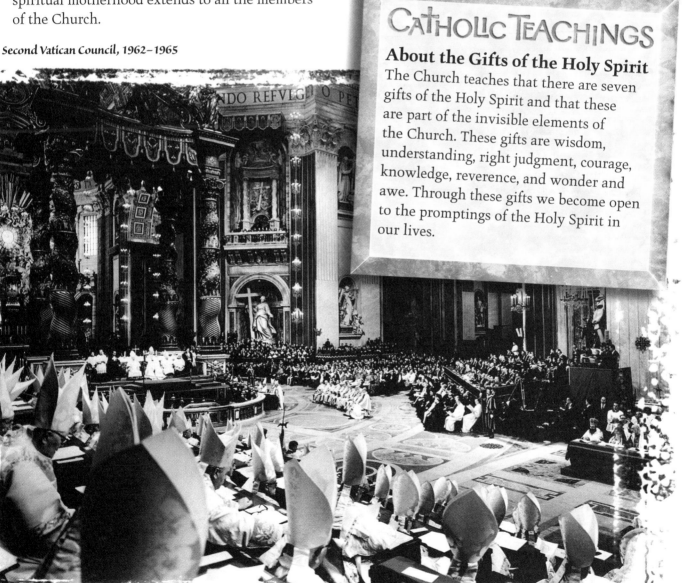

CATHOLIC TEACHINGS
About the Gifts of the Holy Spirit
The Church teaches that there are seven gifts of the Holy Spirit and that these are part of the invisible elements of the Church. These gifts are wisdom, understanding, right judgment, courage, knowledge, reverence, and wonder and awe. Through these gifts we become open to the promptings of the Holy Spirit in our lives.

The Catholic Church

Look again at the elements of the Church. Each must be present in Christ's Church. And where do we find that Church of Christ? The bishops of the council gave a clear answer. They said that the Church of Christ can be found in its essential fullness in the Catholic Church. This is what they taught:

> This is the unique Church of Christ which in the Creed we avow as one, holy, catholic, and apostolic. . . . This Church, constituted and organized in the world as a society, subsists in the Catholic Church, which is governed by the successor of Peter and by the bishops in union with that successor, although many elements of sanctification and of truth can be found outside her visible structure.
> *Church*, 8

The council teaching is that the Church of Christ "subsists" in the Catholic Church. This means that the Church of Christ is truly present in its essential completeness in the Catholic Church. However, as the bishops pointed out, some of the elements of the Church are present in other Christian Churches and communities. For example, all Christians accept and revere Scripture. All Christians are received into the body of Christ through Baptism and enjoy the life of sanctifying grace. Not all Christians, however, continue fully in the apostolic life of the Church under the leadership of the pope and bishops, the successors of the apostles. Nor do all of them have the seven sacraments.

What does this council teaching about the Catholic Church have to do with our daily lives? Everything! That is why we will spend the rest of this chapter trying to understand its importance.

Something Special

If somebody asked you to give the best definition of a precious jewel, such as an emerald, it would not be an easy task. That is because there would be so much to say about the luster and beauty of the gem, its many sides and reflective powers. So it is with the Catholic Church. It, too, has so many aspects that it is difficult to capture all of them in just a few words. However, based on what we have already studied, we can begin to build a helpful definition of the Catholic Church.

We can say that the *Catholic Church* is the community of those who follow Jesus Christ, the community that:

- professes belief in Jesus Christ, the Son of God and risen Lord
- publicly affirms its belief in Christ through Baptism
- celebrates that faith through the Eucharist and other sacraments
- accepts the teachings of Christ that have come down from the time of the apostles
- carries out the sacramental life and mission of the Church under the leadership of those ordained in apostolic succession, that is, the pope and other bishops, together with their priests and deacons.

This definition of the Catholic Church summarizes the key elements of the Church of Christ, both visible and invisible. This is the Church that we experience in our local parish and diocese. This is the Church that we experience when we gather together around the Lord's table to celebrate the Eucharist. This is the Church that exists all over the world. This is also the Church that receives from Christ our Savior "the fullness of the means of salvation" (*Catechism*, 830).

Can there be any doubt, then, that the Catholic Church is something special and that we are privileged to be members of it?

Practical Matters

Knowing how special it is to be a Catholic, we need to ask an important question: What is our relationship to other Christians? Catholics should make no mistake about it. We accept all other Christians as our brothers and sisters in Christ. The Second Vatican Council taught that the Catholic Church accepts other Christians "with respect and affection" (*Ecumenism*, 3).

Nevertheless we do not believe that the Catholic Church and other Christian Churches are all the same. There are differences in belief, practice, and Church organization that separate us. We do not share unity now, but it is our hope that one day all of Christ's followers will be united as one. This is the hard work of ecumenism. *Ecumenism* refers to the effort on the part of Catholics and other Christians to work toward full unity among all baptized people around the world.

A nonbeliever asks you, "What makes the Catholic Church special?" What would your answer be?

To achieve unity, we try to pray and work together with other Christians. But true unity can never be attained if we ignore the real differences that separate us. Take the Eucharist, for example. Unlike some other Christians, Catholics believe that Christ is truly present in the Eucharist and that the Eucharist is a sign of unity. That is why those who do not share our faith are not invited to receive Communion when they visit and attend our celebrations of the Mass. The reception of Holy Communion is a sign of the unity we have in faith, life, and worship within our Catholic community. To share Communion with those not united with us would deny what is really true—that we are not yet one in faith.

In the same way Catholics may not receive communion in Churches that do not share with us our belief in the real presence and that do not have the sacrament of Holy Orders or the apostolic succession of bishops. Without these vital elements we cannot accept their communion as a valid sacrament. To do so would be to deny our belief in the sacramental system of the Church.

There are other occasions as well when we will need to look carefully at the special nature of our Catholic life and faith. Take, for example, marriage between Catholics and non-Catholics. The Church asks the couple planning such a marriage to spend serious time in thought and preparation before taking this important step. The Church, while respecting the faith of the non-Catholic party, asks the Catholic to reaffirm his or her faith. In addition the Catholic is asked to do all in his or her power to see that the children of this marriage are brought up as Catholics. This makes sense, of course. If being a member of the Catholic Church is so important, then all Catholics will want to share their faith with their children.

Think of some ways that you can grow in a deeper appreciation of your Catholic faith.

Scripture UPDATE

If anything is clear in the gospels, it is the close relationship Christ had with his apostles. They were the foundation upon which he built his Church. Our link to Christ and his mission is through the bishops, the successors to the apostles. This apostolic succession of the bishops is an important part of the apostolic succession of the whole Church.

Imagine that you as a Catholic have been invited to a cousin's wedding. Your cousin is not a Catholic, and the ceremony will be held at a Protestant Church. Your cousin hopes that you will receive communion at the ceremony. What would you say to help your cousin understand what you will do?

Someone says to you that ecumenism demands that Christian Churches should discuss only those things they agree on or share and should avoid any difficult topics. Your response?

Each year the Church sets aside a week to pray for Christian unity. However, our parishes can pray and work for unity throughout the year. What do you think young people your age can do to contribute to the ecumenical movement in your neighborhood? Brainstorm several ideas.

YOU ARE MY WITNESSES

Things to Think About

Name and explain two visible and two invisible elements of the Church.

Give the most complete definition of the Catholic Church that you can.

WORDS to REMEMBER

Find and define:

visible elements of the Church

_____

_____

_____

_____

CATHOLICISM: A WAY OF LIFE

You are "a chosen race, a royal priesthood, a holy nation, a people of his own."

1 Peter 2:9

ARE you an important member of the Church? Does what you do really make a difference? What do you think?

74

The Laity

Something wonderful happens when people are baptized and become members of the Church. From that very moment they are changed forever. At Baptism we become not only new creations in Christ and share in God's own life, but we are called to a new way of life. We are called to join in the mission of Christ to the world.

How do Catholics live this new way of life? Basically in one of three ways: Some people become members of religious orders and communities. Others are called to live as ordained ministers. But most of the baptized live their Catholic lives as members of the laity—that is, as laypeople.

As laypeople our way of life begins in and revolves around the parish. There we receive the sacraments of initiation: Baptism, Confirmation, and Eucharist. There we celebrate the sacrament of Reconciliation for the first time. In the parish we continue our instruction in faith that was begun by our parents. We learn more about Jesus, his Church, and what it means to be a Catholic in today's challenging world.

Years later we may celebrate the sacrament of Matrimony in our parish church and begin to journey down a new path in life. It is in the parish as well that we say farewell for the last time to those we love at the celebration of a Christian funeral. Truly the parish is our home in the Catholic Church from the first moment of our lives until the last.

The sacramental life and religious instruction are truly important, but parish life doesn't end there. A parish offers many opportunities for the laity to serve Christ. That is why the first thing that Catholics do when they move into a neighborhood is to register in, or join, the local parish. By adding their names and addresses to the list of parishioners, they become part of the local Catholic family.

It is in the parish that Catholics discover many opportunities to serve others. All their talents can be used in one way or another in various parish committees, organizations, or ministries. For example, laymen and laywomen may be called to serve on the parish council or finance committee. Others may become involved in religious education or take up the work of sharing faith with others in programs of Christian initiation.

Many people feel called to various outreach programs in a parish. These include ministry to the sick or homebound and to those in need of food, clothing, or shelter. Others find that they can serve through involvement with the liturgy. They help to plan liturgies and participate in the liturgical celebrations in their roles as altar servers, members of choirs, leaders of song, musicians, lectors, and extraordinary ministers of the Eucharist.

Some laypeople travel halfway around the globe to serve as missionaries in other lands. Others do mission work in our own country, serving wherever the need is the greatest. Today more than ever before, qualified laypeople are taking leadership positions in dioceses and local parishes. Working closely with the bishop, priests, and deacons, laypeople are putting their talents to work in many ways.

In recent times the Holy Spirit has renewed our understanding of the dignity and importance of the laity in the Church. Now more than ever before the laity are sharing in pastoral ministry as team members. It is exciting to see.

While all this is true, we know that the majority of laypeople carry on the mission of the Church each day by sharing the good news of Christ in the workplace. They use their gifts in their occupations and professions to change the world by the light of the gospel. In all they do, they try to bring to their surroundings the love and justice that is characteristic of God's kingdom.

Jesus himself sent disciples other than the Twelve to join in his saving mission and to prepare the way for him. He once sent out seventy-two to many towns. He reminded them, "The harvest is abundant but the laborers are few; so ask the master of the harvest to send out laborers for his harvest" (Luke 10:2).

Discuss some ways that young people can serve the Church in their parishes.

Religious

Although the laity are the largest group of people in the Church, many thousands of Catholics live out their lives in a different way. These are the members of religious orders and communities. How did this way of life come about?

Throughout the history of the Church, certain men and women have tried to follow Christ in a special way. These are people such as Benedict, Francis of Assisi, Elizabeth Seton, and Teresa of Calcutta. So attractive are their lives and relationships with God that many people have wanted to imitate them. Communities developed around these holy people. Eventually the Church reviewed their way and rules of life and approved them as religious orders and communities. Today these communities are spread throughout the world. How do they live, and what do they do? Let's look more closely at this unique way of living the Catholic life.

All religious share in the joy of community life, ministry, and prayer.

Evangelical Counsels   Religious men and women consecrate themselves to God by vowing to practice poverty, chastity, and obedience. These are known as the *evangelical counsels* because they reflect a gospel way of life. By living these counsels, religious try to follow Christ's example.

- *Poverty* means that a religious man or woman owns no property and tries to live a simple lifestyle. Without seeking wealth or status, a religious gives witness to our total dependence on God and our deep respect for the proper use of this world's goods.

- *Chastity* means that a religious man or woman lives a life of purity as a witness to the kingdom of God. It includes a life of celibacy, which means not marrying. In trying to imitate Jesus in this way, religious want to be free to share God's love with the greatest number of people.

- *Obedience* means that religious men and women choose to listen carefully to God's direction in their lives. Obedience to the Church and to their religious superior means that individual religious are ready to serve God and the Church anywhere.

Community Life   The vowed life of religious is not easy, but it is filled with joy. The vows themselves are positive ways of following Christ's example. The close bonds that religious form in their own community enable them to live their vows fully each day. This is what we mean by a community life. The religious community is truly an individual's religious family.

Some communities are made up of vowed men who also become priests. Some communities are made up of vowed women, whom we call religious sisters. Still others are made up of vowed men who do not become priests. They are known as religious brothers.

CATHOLIC ID

There are two kinds of priests. A *religious priest* is a member of a religious order or community and professes the vows of poverty, chastity, and obedience. He serves anywhere in the world his superiors assign him. A *diocesan priest* is ordained for a particular diocese. With the bishop he dedicates his life to the care of the people of that diocese. He is not a religious nor does he profess the vows of a religious. A diocesan priest does, however, make a promise of celibacy. He also promises obedience to his bishop.

Active religious communities combine a life of prayer with a life of active service. They take part in all aspects of the Church's life. They sponsor and staff schools and hospitals, serve as missionaries, give retreats, work in parishes, and engage in many other ministries. Wherever there is a need in the Church, active religious are ready to go. You may know of some active communities, such as the Jesuits, Franciscan men and women, the Sisters of Mercy, and the Marist Brothers.

Religious communities come in all shapes and sizes. Some have a long history; some are very recent. No matter what, these communities are one of God's great blessings to the Church.

What qualifications do you think a person needs to join a religious community?

Contemplative or Active   There are differences among religious communities. In *contemplative religious communities* men and women dedicate themselves entirely to a life of prayer. They willingly separate themselves from the busyness of the world. They pray constantly for all the members of the Church, but their lives remain hidden from us. That is why they are called contemplatives. In many ways these men and women are the powerhouses of prayer for the entire Church. You may know of some contemplative religious communities, such as the Trappists, the Poor Clares, and the Carmelites.

Name the three vows taken by religious men and women. Explain each one.

Discuss some ministries in which laypeople serve. What can young laypeople do?

We know that the Church is both human and divine. Sometimes, however, we may see too much of the human side of the Church when we hear about the mistakes and weaknesses of Church members — laity, religious, or clergy. What should we do? Think of all the times we can pray for one another, especially at Mass. Use these times to help build up the Church and to grow in love for the Church.

YOU ARE MY WITNESSES

Things to Think About

Why do you think it is important for laity and religious to work together in the Church?

In your opinion what are the most exciting ways that laypeople can serve in the Church?

WORDS to REMEMBER

Find and define:

laity

_____

_____

_____

_____

CHAPTER 10

THE WHOLE CATHOLIC CHURCH

I am the vine, you are the branches.
Whoever remains in me and I in him
will bear much fruit, because
without me you can do nothing.

John 15:5

SOME people think that all Catholics do everything the same way. They think that all Catholics pray at Mass in exactly the same way and follow the same liturgical year. But that is not true.

What is true is that the Church is one in its faith. But it is extremely diverse in the ways that faith is lived and practiced.

Do you know that the whole Catholic Church is made up of twenty-two distinct Catholic Churches in communion with one another? In this chapter we are going to discover that the Church's life is rich and diverse.

Clergy

The membership of the Catholic Church is made up of laity, religious, and clergy. Everyone in the Church belongs to one of these groups. Each group is an important part of our Catholic way of life.

All the Churches of the Catholic Church share in common an ordained leadership called the clergy. These are the bishops, priests (presbyters), and deacons who are empowered by God to exercise authority in the Church. They do this for the service of God's people, each according to his rank in the sacrament of Holy Orders.

The clergy dedicate their lives to the work of Christ and his Church. The priest is the coworker of the bishop in the work of teaching, governing, and sanctifying. Priests, therefore, are never to work independently of the bishop. Rather, they are his representatives in the pastoral care of God's people. Although deacons do not share in the priesthood, as bishops and priests do, they are ordained for a ministry of service.

What about other titles of the clergy, such as cardinal, archbishop, and monsignor? These titles are given to bishops and priests who carry on a special work for the Church or as a special honor. Cardinals and archbishops are bishops; monsignors are priests.

*Msgr. Hartman and Rabbi Gellman
on Good Morning America*

The pope himself is a bishop, the bishop of Rome. As the successor of Peter, he is the head of the college of bishops. In fact the pope has supreme authority over the whole Church. He can make decisions independently of the other bishops but not against or apart from them. This is because the pope and all the other bishops are united in a sacred college.

If someone asked you the purpose of the ordained leadership of the Church, could you give a one-word answer?

CATHOLIC TEACHINGS

About Infallibility

Does infallibility extend to all areas of knowledge? Absolutely not! It has to do only with matters of faith and morals. It has nothing to do with matters of science or other areas of human knowledge. You may be familiar with the story of Galileo. A long time ago the Church misunderstood the work of this great scientist. It mistakenly condemned his scientific teachings about the universe. Today, of course, we know better, and the Church has acknowledged its mistake. This kind of mistake, however, has nothing to do with the gift of infallibility.

Official Teachers

In the Church the official teachers with full authority—the authority of Christ himself—are the pope and the other bishops. They are the official teachers for the whole Church. We call them the *magisterium*, from the Latin word for "teacher."

The teaching office of the magisterium is carried out in two ways. The *ordinary magisterium* is the day-to-day teaching of the pope and bishops about the truths of our faith. Sometimes, however, the pope and bishops teach in a very solemn and formal way. This is called the *extraordinary magisterium*. It happens when the pope gathers all the bishops of the world together at an ecumenical (worldwide) council. Or it happens when the pope by himself makes a solemn and extraordinary pronouncement about our faith.

Jesus promised to be with his Church always, even to the end of the world. He sent the Holy Spirit to teach it and preserve it in the truth (John 16:13). That is why it is unthinkable that the Church, the body of Christ, could fall into error in matters of faith and morality. This is a great gift to the Church.

Catholics have a special name for this gift. That name is infallibility. *Infallibility* is the gift of the Holy Spirit that keeps the whole Church from error—in believing and in teaching—in matters concerning revelation and the deposit of faith. This is the divine guarantee we have that the Church can never be in error about the truths necessary for our salvation.

How is the gift of infallibility exercised in the official teaching office of the Church? It happens only in teaching about matters of faith and morals:

- when the bishops, spread around the world in their own dioceses and in union with the pope, teach the truths of our faith with one voice.
- when the bishops of the world, gathered together by the pope in an ecumenical council, define a truth of our faith.
- when the pope speaks to the whole Church on a matter of faith and morals with the full authority he has as successor of Saint Peter. When the pope does this, he is speaking, not as an individual bishop, but as the pastor of the whole Church. This exercise of infallibility by the pope alone is rare.

What a wonderful thing it is to know that the Holy Spirit is guiding the Church.

Imagine that the Holy Father has called an ecumenical council and that it will begin in the near future. What do you think the world's bishops will talk about?

A Communion of Churches

The Catholic Church's way of life is rich and diverse. As the people of God, Catholics are one, but this unity does not mean that we are all alike. Our Church spreads across every culture and includes many different peoples.

How did this wonderful diversity come to be? As the first Christian communities were founded during the apostolic age, many developed their own unique customs, laws, and practices. Later the Church spread across the Roman Empire. As the empire split into eastern and western sections, differences among the various Churches became more apparent. The Church of the West became known as the Latin, or Western, Catholic Church. The Churches of the East became known as the Eastern Catholic Churches.

The Eastern Catholic Churches should not be confused with the Eastern Orthodox Churches. The Orthodox Churches separated themselves from union with the pope in A.D. 1054 and are not part of the Catholic Church.

Although the Western Church and the Eastern Catholic Churches had many differences, their fundamental beliefs remained the same. Through apostolic succession each had seven sacraments, the threefold ministry (bishop, priest, and deacon), and the same creeds. All of them acknowledged the bishop of Rome, the successor of Peter, as the head of the Church.

Today the whole Catholic Church is made up of twenty-two distinct Catholic Churches in communion with one another and the bishop of Rome. Each of the twenty-two Churches observes one of the Rites of the Church. A *Rite* is a distinctive tradition of liturgy, laws, and customs that expresses the one Catholic faith in its own unique way. There are six different Rites that are practiced by the twenty-two Churches of the Catholic Church.

Most Catholics in the United States follow the Latin Rite. However, Latin Rite Catholics should realize that they can attend Mass (usually called the Divine Liturgy in Eastern Catholic Churches) in any of the other twenty-one Catholic Churches. They may also receive the sacraments there.

Pope John Paul II with a Byzantine Catholic bishop

Christ and His Church

Just as Jesus brought humanity the fullness of God, so the Church brings the fullness of Christ to the world. Jesus Christ, then, lives on in his Church. The Church is really like a sacrament; it makes Christ visible to the world. Jesus' mission is the mission of the Church. The kingdom of God that Jesus preached is the kingdom that the Church seeks to bring about. All this reminds us that the Church is necessary for our salvation, for it is there that we meet Christ our Savior.

Is the Church perfect? No, only God is perfect. Will the Church last? If the Church were merely of human origin, it would never last. But if it comes from God, no one can stop it (Acts 5:38–39). After two thousand years, no one has!

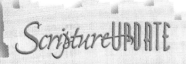

Scripture UPDATE

The Letter to the Colossians summarizes what it means to be a member of the Church: "Whatever you do, in word or in deed, do everything in the name of the Lord Jesus, giving thanks to God the Father through him" (3:17).

The accompanying chart lists the names of all twenty-two Churches and the Rites followed by each. It will help you to appreciate even more the beauty and richness of the Catholic Church.

The Catholic Church	
Churches	**Rites**
1. Latin Catholic Church	This Church follows the Latin (Roman) Rite.
2. Belorussian Catholic Church 3. Bulgarian Catholic Church 4. Greek Catholic Church 5. Hungarian Catholic Church 6. Italo-Albanian Catholic Church 7. Melkite Catholic Church 8. Romanian Catholic Church 9. Ruthenian Catholic Church 10. Slovak Catholic Church 11. Ukrainian Catholic Church 12. Krizevci Catholic Church 13. Albanian Catholic Church 14. Russian Catholic Church	These thirteen Churches follow the Byzantine (Constantinopolitan) Rite.
15. Chaldean Catholic Church 16. Malabar Catholic Church	These two Churches follow the Chaldean Rite.
17. Coptic Catholic Church 18. Ethiopian Catholic Church	These two Churches follow the Alexandrian Rite.
19. Syrian Catholic Church 20. Maronite Catholic Church 21. Syro-Malankara Catholic Church	These three Churches follow the Antiochine Rite.
22. Armenian Catholic Church	This Church follows the Armenian Rite.

Try to find out where the homelands of some of these Churches are. For example, most Catholics in Lebanon belong to the Maronite Catholic Church.

How would you go about explaining to someone that Catholicism is really a way of life?

Someone says to you that laypeople cannot be missionaries in the Church. What would you say in response?

Did you know that your name is officially inscribed in the Catholic Church? It is! In the parish where you were baptized, your name was written down in the parish records and will remain there. This parish is your "home base" in the Catholic Church. Whenever you need a copy of your baptismal certificate, you must contact that parish. Do you know in which parish you were baptized? Remember it always!

YOU ARE MY WITNESSES

Things to Think About

What do we mean when we say that the Catholic Church is a communion of Churches?

Why should we consider infallibility as a gift from God?

Words to Remember

Find and define:

magisterium

_____

_____

_____

_____

THE CHURCH ON ITS WAY

For here we have no
lasting city, but we seek
the one that is to come.

Hebrews 13:14

WHAT dreams do you have for the future?
What dreams do you think God has for our future?

The Pilgrim Church

From the time of the apostles, the Church has been part of every age. It has grown and developed and spread around the world. It is here, but it is not yet complete. The Church is on its way: It is the pilgrim Church.

Why do we call it the pilgrim Church? The Church is like a pilgrim walking in Christ's footsteps in the world. On this pilgrimage we, the people of God, are invited to go along with Christ. He is headed toward the final stage of completing the Church. That stage takes us to the fulfillment of God's kingdom, when Jesus will bring us home with him forever. This pilgrimage, however, is not a free ride. Between today and the last day of the world, there is a great deal to be done to get the world ready for Christ. He is coming again.

The Last Day

Jesus' first coming was at his birth. His *second coming* will be at the end of the world. This second coming is also called the last day, or the day of judgment. The last day will be the end of the world and life as we know it. At that moment the whole magnificent plan of God will be complete. Everything will change. The world we know, with its clouds, mountains, city streets, and country roads, will no longer be the same. All the things we are concerned about now—falling in love, taking a test, getting ill, having fun, even death itself—will come to an end as we know them. Then Christ and his faithful followers will be united forever; the Church will be completed.

When Christ comes, we shall see him for ourselves. What we believed without seeing will then become clear, and we will go on forever with the risen Christ, our brother and our Lord. A timeless, changeless new world will be ours. It seems almost unimaginable, but words such as *time* and *change* will no longer have meaning for us. That's how different everything will be.

For those in heaven there will not be the least chance of being unhappy, lonely, uncertain, or troubled again in any way. What is heaven? *Heaven* is life with the Blessed Trinity forever. It is the state of supreme happiness in which those who have been faithful to God and his commandments will enjoy the beatific vision, seeing God "face-to-face." Jesus himself told us, "I will see you again, and your hearts will rejoice, and no one will take your joy away from you" (John 16:22).

Those in hell, on the other hand, will be miserable for all eternity. *Hell* is eternal separation from God. Hell is the just punishment for those who have rejected God. For those who deliberately choose a life of sin, there is nothing ahead but everlasting misery.

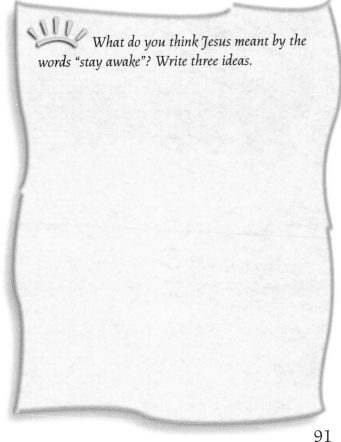

What do you think Jesus meant by the words "stay awake"? Write three ideas.

When will all this happen? Jesus did not say. It wasn't his Father's wish that he make that detail known. How will the world end? We aren't sure. We know only that Jesus put us on alert. He said, "Stay awake, for you know neither the day nor the hour" (Matthew 25:13).

Should we be afraid of this last day and worry that everything will be destroyed? Not at all. God has promised us that it will be the beginning of new life, the likes of which we have never experienced. At his second coming Christ will take possession of creation for his Father and remake it. We read in 2 Peter 3:13: "According to his promise we await new heavens and a new earth."

On that day Jesus will come in glory as king and judge, sitting on a throne surrounded by angels. Everyone who ever existed will be assembled before him. Those whom he has placed on his right will enjoy "eternal life"; those on his left will go off to "eternal punishment" (Matthew 25:31–46). The message is clear; the way we live our lives is up to us.

Do you ever think of yourself as a pilgrim? Where are you headed? Who goes with you? What hopes do you have about your destination?

The choice we make between living for heaven or living for hell will be made known before the whole world on the last day, the day of judgment. On the day of judgment, everyone who ever lived will be present together. Then all will know where they stand in relation to one another and to Christ. This is the *last judgment* that will accompany Christ's second coming at the end of the world. It is described with powerful imagery in Scripture.

CATHOLIC TEACHINGS

About Death

Even though death is a time of great sadness, Catholics have a sure hope in the resurrection. Everything we do points to this hope. We gather to support one another at a wake service and kneel at the coffin to pray for the deceased. Our funeral liturgy is filled with the good news of eternal life. We bury the body with reverence in blessed ground. We continue to pray for our loved ones after their death. We believe what we say in the liturgy: "Lord, for your faithful people life is changed, not ended."

Our Personal Last Day

Human beings have a limited time on earth. Death is a part of our life; it is a result of original sin. In every person's life there is a "last day," and this last day takes place before Christ's second coming. This personal last day is the day we die.

At the time of our death, we shall see ourselves as we are. We will be judged on the choices we have made in the light of Christ's teachings. By the way we live now, we choose heaven or hell. Free people have to accept the responsibility and the consequences of their choices. God does not choose heaven or hell for any one of us; we choose it for ourselves.

For those who have served Christ, death will be the day they have been waiting for—the end of their earthly pilgrimage and the beginning of endless happiness and peace. Will this eternal happiness start immediately? No. For many there must first be a process of purification, which the Church calls purgatory. *Purgatory* is a process of final purification after death in which those who have died in the state of grace grow in the holiness they need to enter the joy of heaven. We can help the souls experiencing purgatory by our good works and prayers, especially the Mass. That is because the souls in purgatory are certain of heaven, unlike those who have chosen hell.

The day of death is final. On that day, in what is called the *particular judgment*, Christ will judge the choice each individual has made and will determine the eternal reward or punishment that each choice deserves. This choice and its consequence—heaven or hell—is what will be repeated before the whole world at the last judgment at the end of the world.

People of faith should not get nervous at the mention of heaven, hell, and judgment. Heaven actually begins on earth with Baptism and is completed in eternity. Because we trust in God's great love and mercy, the Church reminds us that staying out of hell is not our life's work. Staying in heaven is.

Did you ever think that heaven or hell is your choice to make? What do you think about this freedom you have to choose?

The Resurrection of the Dead

Our profession of faith concludes with our belief in the resurrection of the dead on the last day. Catholics firmly proclaim that just as Christ rose from the dead, so will Christ raise us up. On the last day our souls will be reunited with our bodies. Jesus himself scolded some people who did not believe in the resurrection of the dead (Mark 12:24). Jesus also described himself as the "resurrection and the life" (John 11:25). Several times he even gave a sign of the future by bringing some of the dead back to life.

The resurrection of the body is difficult for some people to accept. After all, the body decays after burial, and some bodies are even cremated. What do we say about this? We respond in faith. Just as Christ rose from the dead with his human body totally transformed, so he promised that we will rise at the end of time with our bodies transformed. How will this happen? Through God's almighty power, which is beyond our imagination and understanding.

What we can say with certainty is that we belong completely to Christ. From the moment of Baptism, we are united with him, both body and soul. Because human beings are not just souls, both the body and the soul should experience the rewards or punishments of eternal life.

A Catholic View

You may have heard someone say, "In my next life, I want to be...." What should a Catholic say to this? The Church's teachings about the last things are definite and clear and come from what God has revealed to us. After our pilgrimage of life on earth is ended, God will not make us live another earthly life or a series of earthly lives. We will die only once and then stand before the God of justice, mercy, and love. That is why Catholics do not believe in reincarnation. The idea is totally contrary to God's plan for us.

You may also have heard people who claim to know when and how the world will end. They quote passages from Scripture that seem to say the world will end in complete destruction, with stars and planets falling from the sky. What should a Catholic's reaction be?

As always we turn to the Church to guide us. Just as Catholics see the truth of creation described in poetic terms in Scripture, so, too, the end of time is described in a poetic but truthful way. God is not a God of destruction; he is a God of love. As we already know, there will be new heavens and a new earth. The Church really does have a beautiful and hope-filled view of the end of time and eternal life.

How should our beliefs in the last things affect our daily lives? Do these beliefs frighten you? challenge you? give you hope? Explain.

What is the difference between the last judgment and the particular judgment?

What do we Catholics believe about the resurrection of the dead?

OnLine WITH THE PARISH

In many parishes, bells and chimes call people to worship, remind them of the time of day, and give praise to God. Very often at funerals, bells toll slowly and solemnly to honor the deceased person. Whenever you hear bells tolling during a funeral liturgy, remember that you, too, can pray for that person.

YOU ARE MY WITNESSES

Things to Think About

Some people may say to us that the Catholic Church only looks backward. Knowing what you know about the pilgrim Church, what would you say?

Suppose people tell you that they know all about the end of the world. They claim that, according to the Bible, the end is coming next year. What would you say to them? Does the Bible give us the exact details about the end of the world?

Words to Remember

Find and define:

heaven

_____

_____

_____

_____

CHAPTER 12

DISCIPLES FOREVER

Come, follow me.

Matthew 4:19

THE words of an old hymn remind us:

Whether the road be brief or long,
Whether silent or full of song
We follow, Lord, through night and day:
You are Companion, Light, and Way.

We Christians are pilgrims on our way to fullness of life with God forever.
We do not travel alone, however. We have one another.
We have the Church. Angels and saints walk with us.
The Mother of God protects and supports us.
And Jesus himself is our "Companion, Light, and Way."

Do you believe this? How does it help you during difficult times?

The Morning Star

A study of the Church and what it means to live a Catholic way of life would be incomplete without mentioning Mary, the mother of Jesus. On earth her life was an example of the Church's pilgrimage of faith. In heaven she is the image of what the Church hopes to be. That is why she has been given the beautiful title of the "Morning Star" in the Litany of the Blessed Virgin Mary. She is a guiding light to the pilgrim Church on its way.

Who is this woman for whom thousands of parish churches are named and whose image we see in millions of statues and paintings throughout the world? Why do Catholics show her such great honor and devotion?

There has never been anyone quite like Mary. From all eternity God chose her to be the mother of his Son. For that reason God gave her the privilege of being free from original sin from the first moment of her conception in her mother's womb. This privilege of Mary is what we know as the *immaculate conception*. It doesn't mean that Mary wasn't fully human. It means that she experienced redemption from the first moment of her life. She was full of grace. This was appropriate because she was to be the mother of the Savior of the world. She would carry God's only Son in her womb for nine months.

How did Mary become the mother of God's only Son? At the annunciation she said yes to God's invitation, and she conceived through the power of the Holy Spirit. Her son was not conceived through sexual relations, as other children are. Jesus was to have no human father, but only his Father in heaven. That is why we call Joseph the foster father of Jesus. That is also why we call Mary a virgin and why Jesus' birth is described as a virgin birth. Mary never engaged in sexual relations at any time in her life.

As we already know, the child born of the Virgin Mary was a divine Person with both a human nature and a divine nature. For that reason the greatest title of Mary is Mother of God. Jesus was not a human person; he was a divine Person with two natures.

And that is why the Church reminds us that Mary must always be seen in relationship to her son. Mary's greatness comes from Christ. The Church's teaching is clear: "What the Catholic faith believes about Mary is based on what it believes about Christ, and what it teaches about Mary illumines in turn its faith in Christ" (*Catechism*, 487).

The Litany of the Blessed Virgin Mary prays to Mary under many titles. They include Mother most pure, Cause of our joy, House of gold, Health of the sick, Queen of peace. Write a prayer using one title, or draw a symbol that expresses it for you.

The First Disciple

Who knew Jesus better than Mary did? We know from Scripture that she was an intimate part of Jesus' life. She brought him into the world. Like other mothers, she was there as her child grew. She witnessed his public ministry and even stood at the foot of the cross. But her closeness to Jesus did not end there. Along with Jesus' disciples she became a witness to the resurrection and ascension. She also waited in prayerful anticipation for the coming of the Holy Spirit. All these things tell us that Mary was the first of Jesus' disciples. From the moment she agreed to the incarnation, she was a Christian before anyone else was.

Mary cooperated fully with God's grace and remained free of any personal sin her whole life long. She was obedient to whatever God asked of her, and she followed no one but her son. In bringing Jesus into the world and in living as she did, Mary is a true model for the Church. She gives the example all of us should follow. Because we are the body of Christ, Mary, the mother of Jesus, is the Mother of the Church and our mother, too.

Although we do not know all the details of Mary's earthly life, we can be sure that she was a treasured member of the early Christian community. But what became of Mary? The Church teaches that because of her immaculate conception, Mary was given another privilege at the end of her life. She anticipated the resurrection that all of us will experience. Mary was taken up, or assumed, both body and soul into heaven at the end of her earthly life. This is known as the *assumption*.

Jesus loved his mother very much and knew how important she would be for his Church. When he was dying on the cross, Jesus himself said to John, his beloved disciple, and to us, "Behold, your mother" (John 19:27). Having been taken up into heaven, Mary has not forgotten us. She is still Mother of the Church. She is the mother of each one of us.

Some people have described Mary as the perfect disciple of Jesus. Give examples to show why this is so.

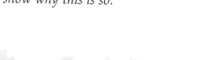

Scripture UPDATE

Mark 3:31–35 and several other Scripture passages refer to the brothers and sisters of Jesus. If Mary was always a virgin, what do these passages mean? The Church teaches us that these passages are "not referring to other children of the Virgin Mary. In fact James and Joseph, 'brothers of Jesus,' are the sons of another Mary, a disciple of Christ, whom Saint Matthew significantly calls 'the other Mary.' They are close relations of Jesus, according to an Old Testament expression" (*Catechism*, 500).

Saint Martin de Porres

Saint Cecilia

Blessed Kateri Tekakwitha

Help Along the Way

Whenever we think of the Blessed Virgin Mary, we should remember that she is the first and greatest among the saints. Who are these men and women called saints? Why are they so important in our Catholic life?

The word *saint* means "one who is holy." It was used in the early Church to describe all the baptized. They were called holy because through Baptism they had been given a share in the divine life. As time passed, however, *saint* was used more often for holy people who followed Christ in extraordinary and heroic ways. For example, the early martyrs, who shed their blood for the faith, were immediately recognized and honored as saints in the communities where they lived.

Eventually an official process was developed to help the entire Church community recognize those who had lived exceptional lives of faith. This process is called *canonization*. How does it work? First the name of a person considered to be worthy of the title saint is submitted to Church authorities.

Then a thorough investigation of this person's life is conducted. When this process is completed and positive results are found, the pope proclaims that person a saint. Now the new saint can be honored by all the members of the Church. We can follow his or her path to holiness.

Are all the saints in heaven canonized? Of course not. Millions upon millions of good and holy people, including members of our own families, have not been officially canonized by the Church but may well be in heaven. The saints who have been canonized are a gift to the whole Church. They have been set before us as heroes and heroines of faith.

The canonized saints are a great treasure. We honor them by remembering them in prayer and by setting aside special feast days to commemorate their lives. Besides this, we name shrines, churches, and other institutions after them and dedicate these structures to their memory. But there is one day during the year when all the saints, both canonized and not canonized, are honored. That day is November 1.

Whenever we think about saints, we are reminded that all the members of the Church are connected with one another through Baptism and faith. This includes three groups: the members of the Church on earth, those experiencing purgatory, and those who have already attained the blessedness of heaven. We call this union of all the Church members the communion of saints. The *communion of saints* is the unity and cooperation of the members of the Church on earth with those in heaven and in purgatory.

Why is this communion of saints so important for us? It reminds us that we can pray for the dead and assist them by our prayers. It also reminds us that Mary and the other saints can pray for us, or intercede for us with God. The saints are our brothers and sisters in faith. Through their prayers for us and by the example of their lives, they are powerful friends in helping the pilgrim Church on its way.

CATHOLIC ID

Every Catholic should know that the Church has its own body of laws called canon law. The word *canon* means an "official rule." The canons of the Church are formulated to guide the life of the Church. Questions they deal with include Church administration, the rights and obligations of the faithful, and the correct procedures for Catholic marriages and other acts of divine worship. There are 1,752 canons, or laws, in the *Code of Canon Law*. There is one code of canon law for the Western Catholic Church and another for the Eastern Catholic Churches.

If you could choose any saint to be your special friend and companion on the way, who would it be? Why?

Living as Catholics

Our study of basic Catholic beliefs has now come to a close. Each day we have an opportunity to make these beliefs a part of our lives. Our beliefs are so important that they truly identify us as members of the Catholic Church.

Our beliefs give meaning to everything we do. What we believe about the life of grace and our need for salvation, for example, affects the choices we make between right and wrong. Knowing about the Blessed Trinity and understanding the importance of Christ and his Church are the foundations of our sacramental life and worship of God. Our understanding of God, revelation, and faith itself helps us to realize that we can have a personal relationship with the transcendent and living God. All our beliefs, in fact, shape our Catholic life each and every day.

As informed members of the Church today, we stand on the shoulders of those who have gone before us in faith. They have passed on to us the teachings of Christ and his Church and have shown us how to live them in a dynamic way. It is now up to us to share these with the whole world.

Things to SHARE

What do you think is Mary's greatest title? Why?

What does your Catholic faith mean to you? What have you learned in this course that has increased your gratitude for your faith?

The Blessed Virgin Mary is so important for the Church that we honor her on many days during the liturgical year. Three of them are celebrated as holy days of obligation. These are: the Immaculate Conception (December 8), Mary, Mother of God (January 1), and the Assumption (August 15). Your parish will announce special Mass schedules for these feasts. Mark these days on your family calendar, and plan to celebrate at Mass.

YOU ARE MY WITNESSES

Things to Think About

What does it mean for you to know that you are a member of the communion of saints and connected with all the other members of the Church, living and dead?

Why is it important for every Catholic to have a deep love and respect for the Blessed Virgin Mary?

WORDS to REMEMBER

Find and define:

communion of saints

_____

_____

_____

_____

BRINGING THE WORLD
TO CHRIST

CHAPTER 13

Through faith you are all children of God in Christ Jesus. For all of you who were baptized into Christ have clothed yourselves with Christ.

Galatians 3:26–27

THE day of our Baptism is a day unlike any other. From the moment of Baptism, we are changed forever. As children of God we are set apart and consecrated to carry on Christ's mission. Do you know the facts about your own Baptism? See how much of your baptismal record you can fill out from memory. Then ask your family to help.

My Baptismal Record

I, _____

the child of _____

and _____

and born on _____
(date)

in _____
(place)

was reborn in the sacrament of Baptism by water
and the Holy Spirit

on _____
(date)

by _____
(priest or deacon)

in _____
(parish community)

_____
(address)

My sponsors were _____

and _____

Chosen by God

When does our responsibility to carry on Christ's mission to the whole world begin? Some people may think that this responsibility begins when we are adults or that it is something for older members of the Church. But that is not true. Recall the story of the prophet Jeremiah.

Jeremiah was a young man when God called him to be a prophet. In response to this call, Jeremiah said to God, "I know not how to speak; I am too young." At this God said to him, "Say not, 'I am too young.' To whomever I send you, you shall go; whatever I command you, you shall speak" (Jeremiah 1:6–7).

God is saying the same thing to each one of us in Christ. As people of faith and as members of the body of Christ, we are appointed right now to share our faith and the good news of the gospel with the whole world. We call this mission of bringing the good news to others evangelization.

Evangelization means bringing the good news to every person and to all parts of the human experience. It means that we bring the world to Christ and Christ to the world. It is something so exciting that when it happens, the lives of people are transformed from within and made new. They begin to see everything with the eyes of Christ.

This does not happen automatically. Rather, it takes initiative, commitment, and hard work. After all, the best witness to Christ and our faith is the way we live our lives. It takes more than good will and intention; we must know Christ and know our faith. That is one of the reasons this course on the creed is so important.

How can you as a young person carry on the work of evangelization? Where will you go? What will you do? Let's begin to explore three areas in which evangelization can happen: at home, in your school and neighborhood, and in the wider world. This will be a journey of discovery. Let us turn to the Holy Spirit and ask him to be our guide.

Looking at Ourselves

Evangelization is so important in the lives of Catholics that our recent popes have talked to us about it many times. But they do not want us to go off unprepared. Like Jesus they have urged us to look at the "signs of the times" (Matthew 16:3) to see where God wants us to work in our world, calling us to be a part of his kingdom.

The first people to be evangelized must be ourselves. Pope Paul VI, for example, said that "the first means of evangelization is the witness of an authentically Christian life" (*On Evangelization*, 41). This means that we have to believe and practice what we are going to share with others. Otherwise our witness becomes empty and unbelievable.

What are the signs of the times in your own life? Let's take a closer look. For example, think about the music you enjoy. What are your favorite songs? Write several of their titles in the space above.

MY FAVORITE SONGS

Why are these songs your favorites? What do the words of the songs tell you about yourself, what you hope for, what you enjoy? Do the words and feelings of these songs help you to live your faith? Do they make you uneasy about your faith?

The answers we give to questions such as these help us to see where faith challenges us. They help us to see where we must allow the gospel and all that we profess about our faith to become real for our lives. Remember Paul's words: "Through faith you are all children of God in Christ Jesus. For all of you who were baptized into Christ have clothed yourselves with Christ" (Galatians 3:26–27).

Do the things you enjoy, such as music, help you to see where you need to clothe yourself in Christ even more? How can your faith become more real in your life? Write your thoughts here.

Family Life

Once we have evangelized ourselves, the first and most obvious people with whom we come into contact are members of our family. Evangelizing, however, doesn't mean that we are going to preach to our family or tell them what to do. What it means is that we are going to try as hard as we can to bring the presence of Christ into our family's life in any way possible. What are the signs of the times in your family's life? Let's take a closer look.

Complete the following statements for yourself:

1. I most enjoy being with my family when

2. The quality I like best about my family is

3. I am most uncomfortable with my family when

4. My family is most uncomfortable with me when

In the chart check off the areas in which you think you need to grow or to work harder as a family evangelizer.

___ gratitude	___ generosity
___ joy	___ anger
___ friendliness	___ patience
___ helpfulness	___ cheerfulness
___ enthusiasm	___ support
___ selfishness	___ stubbornness
___ jealousy	___ prayerfulness
___ cooperation	___ attentiveness
___ responsibility	___ forgiveness

Young people who are well trained in faith and prayer must become more and more the apostles of youth. The Church counts greatly on their contribution.

Pope Paul VI, On Evangelization, 72

Look over your list and your answers. This isn't an examination of conscience or a way to find out how bad we are. This is a way to get in touch with our lives. This is a way to be real evangelizers, to bring the values of the gospel home with us.

The signs of the times are there for us to read. The possibilities of being effective evangelizers are there for us, too.

Behold, I am with you always, until the end of the age (Matthew 28:20).

Think about some things that need to be changed, or transformed, in you so that you can become a true evangelizer and witness to Christ. For example someone might pray:

Transform my <u>laziness</u> into <u>energy to do your work</u>.

What "transformations" do you need?

TRANSFORM

my _____ into _____

my _____ into _____

my _____ into _____

my _____ into _____

my _____ into _____

Here is a prayer to help you see more clearly how to be an effective evangelizer.

Jesus,
you have chosen me
as a member of your Church
to be your evangelizer.
Help me to
see each day where I can
bring the message
of your good news to others.
Help me to
transform my own life
and so be a witness
to my family.
Amen.

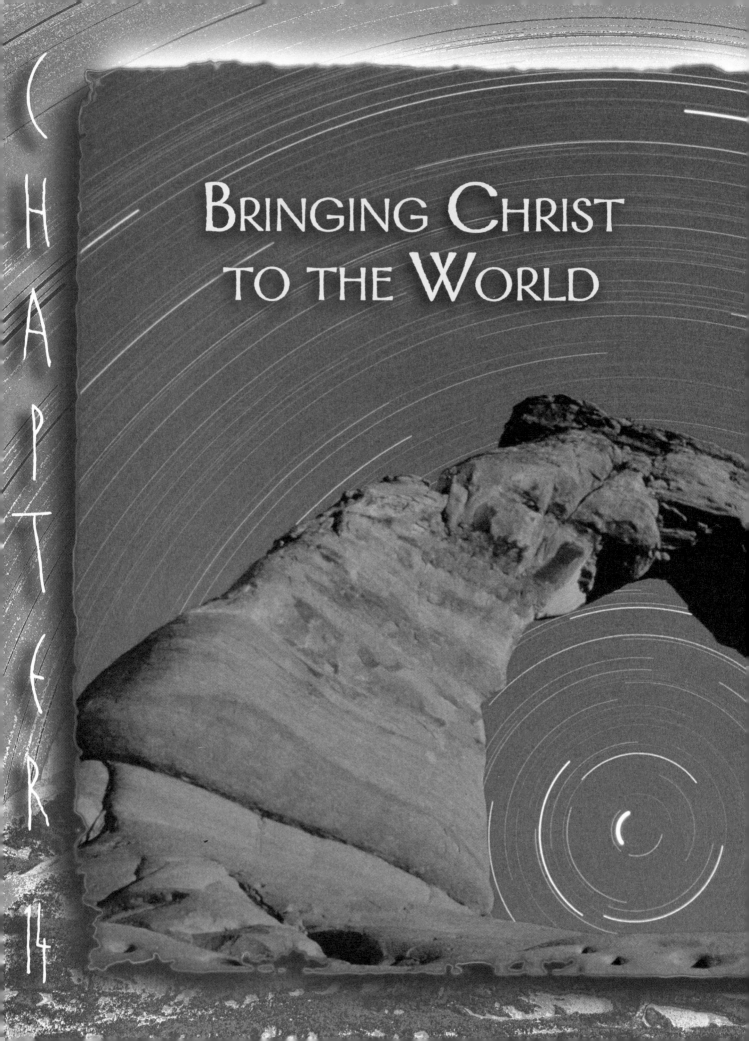

CHAPTER 14

BRINGING CHRIST
TO THE WORLD

You continue to build your
Church with chosen stones,
enlivened by the Spirit,
and cemented together by love.

Prayer for the Dedication of a Church

*The Church has so much to talk about
with youth, and youth have so much
to share with the Church.*

Pope John Paul II, The Lay Faithful, 46

What do you think you have to share with the Church?

Friends

Having good friends is one of the greatest experiences we can ever have in life. Being good friends means that we wish only what is good for the other person — only what will make that person truly happy.

To help us get in touch with friendship, let's take a look at the way friendship is shown in our favorite movies and television programs.

Look over the answers you have written down in these charts. Are you surprised at your answers? How would you compare these answers with what your faith tells you about friendship? Friends can be evangelizers to one another. Do you see any possibility for evangelization here? Write a friendship evangelization plan.

My Friendship Evangelization Plan

Recent Movies I Have Seen

Names of Movies:

What These Movies Tell Me About Friendship:

Favorite Television Programs

Names of Television Programs:

What These Programs Tell Me About Friendship:

School and Neighborhood

Strange as it may seem, the hardest and most challenging place to be an effective evangelizer may very well be in our own backyard. It is always most difficult to evangelize our peers. It may be easier to travel halfway around the world and meet people who have never heard of Christ than to speak with and give witness to him among the people we see and hang out with day after day.

What does this mean? It means that we have to be courageous, imaginative, and skillful in bringing the truth and values of the gospel to this important part of our world. But how do we bring the gospel and the truth of faith to the football or soccer field, to the basketball court, to the mall, to the classroom, or to a Friday night dance? After all, this is the world in which we live every day.

Read the following descriptions, and think about the situations as possible evangelizing opportunities. For each, write one way you would try to bring gospel values to this experience.

Evangelizing Moments

• For many months your parish council has been asking for volunteers of all ages to help start an outreach program to the elderly and the homebound. It is not easy to volunteer alone. What are your plans as an evangelizer?

• Sports have always been important in your school. But lately you and others have noticed a different attitude on the part of many, both young people and adults. Sports and winning seem to have taken over as the most important things in life. What are your plans as an evangelizer?

• The local mall is the place to hang out and meet others. However, the mall security guards have been cracking down in the last couple of months. People were complaining about the noise and rough behavior on the part of some of your peers. What are your plans as an evangelizer?

Look back at what you have written today about being an evangelizer. Are you surprised that evangelization can take place in situations where you might have thought it would not be possible?

A Young Evangelizer Writes

During my senior year at Georgetown University, one of my Jesuit teachers suggested that I volunteer to work in South Africa after graduation. I imagine he thought it would be a good way to round out my education as a Catholic and challenge me as a person of faith. Although his suggestion sounded exciting, I had some other ideas about my life. My life was filled with many blessings, and I wanted to give something back to my own community in the United States. That's how I ended up spending a year in a large U.S. city far from my home. There I taught young people in an inner-city school.

My experience opened my eyes to a part of life I had never really seen. In an area overrun with gangs, drugs, and violence, the strength and ability of my students impressed me deeply. I started out thinking that I could give something back to the community, but I was the one who was actually taught. Now as a law student I am learning to bring greater justice to the inner city.

Tom Sweeney

Another Young Evangelizer Writes

When I was in college, I had the opportunity to visit other countries in Central and South America. There I was shocked to see so many people living in cardboard houses and going hungry. For the first time in my life, I realized just how the poor of the world have to live. As a person of faith and a member of the Church, I knew that I had to do something about this.

After college I volunteered to work with a group sponsored by the Ursuline Sisters. This group is called Ursuline Companions in Mission. For the next two years, I found myself working alongside others in youth and prison ministry and family counseling here in the United States. I even went to Central America and worked in an orphanage in Honduras. Was it easy? No. But these experiences helped to change my life. Now as a teacher I try to share with young Catholics and help them see what missionary activity is all about.

Patrice McDermott

The Wider World

You may be surprised where life leads you as an evangelizer. For some it could even be halfway around the world. That's because the work of evangelization and mission is the work of all Church members, not just the clergy and religious. The Church teaches us that through Baptism we are a prophetic and priestly people offering spiritual sacrifices in our lives and announcing Christ to the world. The Church reminds us that "the faithful exercise their baptismal priesthood through their participation, each according to his own vocation, in Christ's mission as priest, prophet, and king" (*Catechism*, 1546).

Now that you have read about their experiences, what questions would you ask these two young Catholics about their evangelizing activities?

What dreams do you have for evangelizing in the wider world?

How can you prepare to help make those dreams come true?

A Prayer for Evangelizers

Leader: On the day of our Baptism, we began a journey of bringing the world to Christ. From that moment we have learned about our faith in Christ and are proud to profess it in his name. Before we renew our baptismal vows, let us listen closely to the word of God.

Reader 1: A reading from the First Letter of Peter (1 Peter 2:3–5, 9–10).

You have tasted that the Lord is good. Come to him, a living stone, rejected by human beings but chosen and precious in the sight of God, and, like living stones, let yourselves be built into a spiritual house to be a holy priesthood to offer spiritual sacrifices acceptable to God through Jesus Christ. You are "a chosen race, a royal priesthood, a holy nation, a people of his own, so that you may announce the praises" of him who called you out of darkness into his wonderful light. Once you were "no people" but now you are God's people.

The word of the Lord.

All: Thanks be to God.

Leader: Now let us renew our baptismal vows that were first made on the day of our Baptism.

Reader 2: Do you reaffirm your renunciation of evil and renew your commitment to Jesus Christ?

All: I do.

Reader 3: Do you believe in God the Father?

All: I believe in God, the Father almighty, creator of heaven and earth.

Reader 4: Do you believe in Jesus Christ, the Son of God?

All: I believe in Jesus Christ, his only son, our Lord.
He was conceived by the power of the Holy Spirit and born of the Virgin Mary.
He suffered under Pontius Pilate, was crucified, died, and was buried.
He descended to the dead.
On the third day he rose again.
He ascended into heaven, and is seated at the right hand of the Father.
He will come again to judge the living and the dead.

Reader 5: Do you believe in the Holy Spirit?

All: I believe in the Holy Spirit,
the holy catholic Church,
the communion of saints,
the forgiveness of sins,
the resurrection of the body,
and the life everlasting.

Reader 6: Will you continue in the apostles'
teaching and fellowship,
in the breaking of bread, and in
the prayers?

All: I will, with God's help.

Reader 7: Will you persevere in resisting evil,
and, whenever you fall into sin,
repent and return to the Lord?

All: I will, with God's help.

Reader 8: Will you proclaim by word and example
the Good News of God in Christ?

All: I will, with God's help.

Reader 9: Will you seek and serve Christ
in all persons,
loving your neighbor as yourself?

All: I will, with God's help.

Reader 10: Will you strive for justice
and peace among all people,
and respect the dignity of every
human being?

All: I will, with God's help.

Leader: May Almighty God,
the Father of our Lord Jesus Christ,
who has given us a new birth by water and
the Holy Spirit,
and bestowed upon us the forgiveness of sins,
keep us in eternal life by his grace,
in Christ Jesus our Lord.

All: Amen.

*Before singing a closing song, each member of the group
comes forward to dip his or her hand in holy water and
make the sign of the cross.*

BLESSED BE GOD.
BLESSED BE HIS HOLY NAME

Blessed be Jesus Christ, true God and true man.
Blessed be the name of Jesus.
Blessed be his most sacred heart.
Blessed be his most precious blood.
Blessed be Jesus in the most holy
  sacrament of the altar.
Blessed be the Holy Spirit, the Paraclete.
Blessed be the great mother of God,
  Mary most holy.
Blessed be her most holy and immaculate
  conception.
Blessed be her glorious assumption.
Blessed be the name of Mary, virgin
  and mother.
Blessed be Saint Joseph, her most chaste spouse.
Blessed be God in his angels and in his saints.

THE DIVINE PRAISES

OUR FATHER,
WHO ART IN HEAVEN,

hallowed be thy name:
thy kingdom come;
thy will be done on earth as it is
in heaven.
Give us this day our daily bread:
and forgive us our trespasses
as we forgive those who trespass
against us;
and lead us not into temptation.
but deliver us from evil.
Amen.

OUR FATHER

HAIL MARY,
FULL OF GRACE,

the Lord is with you!
Blessed are you among women,
and blessed is the fruit of your womb,
 Jesus.
Holy Mary, Mother of God,
pray for us sinners,
now and at the hour of our death.
Amen.

HAIL MARY

MY GOD,
I AM SORRY FOR MY SINS
WITH ALL MY HEART.

In choosing to do wrong
and failing to do good,
I have sinned against you
whom I should love above all things.
I firmly intend, with your help,
to do penance,
to sin no more,
and to avoid whatever leads me to sin.
Our Savior Jesus Christ
suffered and died for us.
In his name, my God, have mercy.

ACT OF CONTRITION

HAIL, HOLY QUEEN,
MOTHER OF MERCY,

hail, our life, our sweetness, and our hope.
To you we cry, the children of Eve:
to you we send up our sighs,
mourning and weeping in this land of exile.
Turn, then, most gracious advocate,
your eyes of mercy toward us;
lead us home at last
and show us the blessed fruit of your womb,
Jesus:
O clement, O loving, O sweet Virgin Mary.

HAIL, HOLY QUEEN

COME, HOLY SPIRIT,
FILL THE HEARTS OF YOUR FAITHFUL.

And kindle in them the fire of your love.

Send forth your Spirit and they shall be created.
And you will renew the face of the earth.

Let us pray.

Lord,
by the light of the Holy Spirit
you have taught the hearts of your faithful.
In the same Spirit
help us to relish what is right
and always rejoice in your consolation.

We ask this through Christ our Lord.
Amen.

PRAYER TO THE HOLY SPIRIT

I BELIEVE IN GOD,
THE FATHER ALMIGHTY,

creator of heaven and earth.
I believe in Jesus Christ, his only Son,
   our Lord.
He was conceived by the power of
   the Holy Spirit
   and born of the Virgin Mary.
He suffered under Pontius Pilate,
   was crucified, died, and was buried.
He descended to the dead.
On the third day he rose again.
He ascended into heaven,
   and is seated at the right hand
   of the Father.
He will come again to judge the living
   and the dead.
I believe in the Holy Spirit,
   the holy catholic Church,
   the communion of saints,
   the forgiveness of sins,
   the resurrection of the body,
   and the life everlasting.
Amen.

APOSTLES' CREED

GLORY TO THE FATHER,
AND TO THE SON,

and to the Holy Spirit:
as it was in the beginning, is now,
   and will be for ever.
Amen.

GLORY TO THE FATHER

WE BELIEVE IN ONE GOD,

THE FATHER, THE ALMIGHTY,

maker of heaven and earth,
of all that is seen and unseen.

We believe in one Lord, Jesus Christ,
the only Son of God,
eternally begotten of the Father,
God from God, Light from Light,
true God from true God,
begotten, not made, one in Being with
the Father.
Through him all things were made.
For us men and for our salvation
he came down from heaven:
by the power of the Holy Spirit
he was born of the Virgin Mary,
and became man.
For our sake he was crucified under
Pontius Pilate;
he suffered, died, and was buried.
On the third day he rose again
in fulfillment of the Scriptures;
he ascended into heaven
and is seated at the right hand of the
Father.
He will come again in glory to judge
the living and the dead,
and his kingdom will have no end.

We believe in the Holy Spirit, the Lord,
the giver of life,
who proceeds from the Father and the
Son.
With the Father and the Son he is
worshiped and glorified.
He has spoken through the Prophets.
We believe in one holy catholic and
apostolic Church.
We acknowledge one baptism for the
forgiveness of sins.
We look for the resurrection of the dead,
and the life of the world to come.
Amen.

NICENE CREED

ETERNAL REST

GRANT UNTO THEM,

O Lord.
And let perpetual light shine upon them.
May they rest in peace.
Amen.
May their souls and the souls of all the
faithful departed, through the mercy of
God, rest in peace.
Amen.

May the angels lead you into paradise;
may the martyrs come to welcome you
and take you to the holy city,
the new and eternal Jerusalem.

PRAYERS FOR THE DECEASED

O LORD, SUPPORT US

ALL THE DAY LONG,

until the shadows lengthen,
and the evening comes,
and the busy world is hushed,
and the fever of life is over,
and our work is done.
Then in your mercy,
grant us a safe lodging,
and a holy rest,
and peace at the last.

John Henry Newman

A NOVEMBER PRAYER

THE BREAD WHICH
YOU DO NOT USE

  Is the bread of the hungry.
The garment hanging in your wardrobe
  Is the garment of one who is naked.
The shoes that you do not wear
  Are the shoes of one who is barefoot.
The money you keep locked away
  Is the money of the poor.
The acts of charity you do not perform
  Are so many injustices you commit.

Saint Basil the Great
A MEDITATION

LORD, I BELIEVE
IN YOU: INCREASE MY FAITH.

I trust in you: strengthen my trust.
I love you: let me love you more and more.
I am sorry for my sins: deepen my sorrow.

I worship you as my first beginning,
I long for you as my last end,
I praise you as my constant helper,
and call on you as my loving protector.

Guide me by your wisdom,
correct me with your justice,
comfort me with your mercy,
protect me with your power.

Attributed to Pope Clement XI
SELECTIONS FROM THE UNIVERSAL PRAYER

LET NOTHING
DISTURB YOU,

nothing cause you fear;
All things pass
God is unchanging.
Patience obtains all:
Whoever has God
Needs nothing else,
God alone suffices.

Saint Teresa of Ávila
REFLECTION ON PATIENCE

THE ANGEL SPOKE
GOD'S MESSAGE TO MARY,

and she conceived of the Holy Spirit.
Hail, Mary. . . .

"I am the lowly servant of the Lord:
let it be done to me according to your word."
Hail, Mary. . . .

And the Word became flesh
and lived among us.
Hail, Mary. . . .

Pray for us, holy Mother of God,
that we may become worthy of the
promises of Christ.

Let us pray.

Lord,
fill our hearts with your grace:
once, through the message of an angel you
revealed to us the incarnation of your Son;
now, through his suffering and death
lead us to the glory of his resurrection.
We ask this through Christ our Lord.
Amen.

THE ANGELUS

THE TEN COMMANDMENTS

1. I am the LORD your God: you shall not have strange Gods before me.

2. You shall not take the name of the LORD your God in vain.

3. Remember to keep holy the LORD's Day.

4. Honor your father and your mother.

5. You shall not kill.

6. You shall not commit adultery.

7. You shall not steal.

8. You shall not bear false witness against your neighbor.

9. You shall not covet your neighbor's wife.

10. You shall not covet your neighbor's goods.

CATECHISM OF THE CATHOLIC CHURCH

~THE~ BEATITUDES

Blessed are the poor in spirit,
  for theirs is the kingdom of heaven.

Blessed are they who mourn,
  for they will be comforted.

Blessed are the meek,
  for they will inherit the land.

Blessed are they who hunger and thirst
    for righteousness,
    for they will be satisfied.

Blessed are the merciful,
  for they will be shown mercy.

Blessed are the clean of heart,
  for they will see God.

Blessed are the peacemakers,
  for they will be called children of God.

Blessed are they who are persecuted
    for the sake of righteousness,
    for theirs is the kingdom of heaven.

Matthew 5:3-10

Index

Italicized numbers refer to definitions   **Bold-faced** numbers refer to chapters

Italicized numbers refer to definitions

Bold-faced numbers refer to chapters